TWIST AND SHOUT

TWIST AND SHOUT

AN AWKWARD LIFE WITH TOURETTE'S

TYLER OBERHEU

ReadersMagnet, LLC

CONTENTS

A WORD FROM THE AUTHOR

I wrote this book in the summer of 2014. Originally it was a journal; created to cope with my paradigm being so shifted it was unrecognizable. From 2011 to 2017, I was in Hell. Frankly I don't even know if I am being literal or figurative. I was on so much medication that the thoughts I had back then aren't mine today, they belong to some doppelganger, an alien mind that I can distantly remember, but would rather not.

Before you read this book, you should be aware that:

- I was 20 years old
- Mentally I was somewhere near 15
- I was on 5 different drugs that were one hundred percent legal but really shouldn't be, derealization is a symptom that I would not wish on my worst enemy.
- I went to DePaul University to study English and Writing after I had already written this book.

That being said, my last point is:

- You will be able to see the difference in my writing ability and style.

I am not even bashing myself for incoherent writing, I have learned so much since writing this book that's it makes me look back at those years with a humbling nostalgia. The summer of 2014 I sat in my house all day, every day, typing away whatever thoughts came into my head. I sat in one room, however I was certainly on a journey.

Even today, five years after I originally sat down to write this, I am looking back through the pages with astonishment. I have taken the liberty to edit these pages, trying my best not to disrupt the image I have tried to create all those years ago.

Originally, this book was published by a Chicago-native company in 2015. Later, they went out of business, prompting me to self-publish under my own name. The only reason you are reading this is because it was resurrected recently, giving new life to old words and dead thoughts and dreams.

On the next page you will read that "I am not the hero of this story", which I still stand by. Reading through the thoughts of a 20 year old Tyler Oberheu, I can clearly see what areas would be best done away with, while still keeping that 20 year old alive. I've written out many real names of friends, many real stories that I simply do not wish anyone to read to protect myself and others, as well as there being a curse word every few sentences. I've kept some in there, however for the sake that obsessive swearing can be a distraction toward the point being made, I thought it was the best idea for a new and improved edition.

Regardless, I do sincerely hope you find this book useful or at least entertaining. Not every writer gets a chance to have others read their story, I am beyond grateful for this ability.

Enjoy.

—*Tyler Oberheu, April 18th 2019.*

TWIST AND SHOUT

I am not the hero of this story.

I am not a positive role model or an expert on this disease or a life coach.

Simply, I am just a guy with a lot of spare time and some things to say.

My name is Tyler Oberheu, and I have Tourette's syndrome.

I assume you do too, or maybe you are the parent of a child with Tourette's or maybe a friend of someone. Or maybe you're just curious about my book and have decided to pick it up and read.

Whatever the matter, a lot of what you thought you knew about this disease is about to change. Let's start off with the beginning: I was diagnosed with Tourette's syndrome at age seventeen. "How is this possible" you say? Well turns out you can get this disease at any time. But let me quiet your alarm and worry for a second. I was diagnosed at age seventeen yet I first started showing symptoms at twelve.

Still though, that's a little old to have this disease.

Ever since that day in my bedroom, when I was showing my friend Jeremy my pet lizard (that may sound strangely sexual but I assure you it's not) and I started coughing. My mom heard me and thought I was sick. Then the coughing kept happening. Then it was throat clearing. Then grunting. Five years later it was a pain in my shoulder and weird arm roll I would do to try to alleviate the alien feeling I was having.

Then came the violent head thrashes and high pitched yelping. Then came the hitting.

My tics have changed over time. If you have this disease then I'm sure that's no strange news to you. If you just started having funny feelings then I afraid to tell you that change is a comin. That could be good or bad. Tics can change from worse to not-as-worse. Anyway there will be more on that later. Throughout this book we will cover many things related to Tourette's and some things that are not so related. I've had many misadventures during my time with this disease. Circumstances that may not have happened had I never gotten sick. If you're a concerned parent then you might be thinking "How will my child be doing in school?" or "Will this upset his or her life THAT much?" and "What can we do to help?" and as a person with Tourette's you may be thinking "How can I make this shit stop?" or something like that.

Join me on this journey as we explore medicine, drugs (both the serious kinds and the fun kinds), school, work, life and the universe. "What the fuck does that have to do with anything" you ask? Well shut up, it's my book, I'll talk about whatever I want. And you're gonna sit there and like it. I mean you could always just stop reading or even return your book from whatever fine establishment you bought it from. But that would be childish don't you think? I mean you're just going to give up before this book even really starts and stop reading now? Isn't that giving up too early? Am I asking too many questions and should just get to the point? Of course it is, but I have to fill out a couple hundred pages of words so I'm going to talk about a lot of stuff that seems unimportant but I assure you it's not. You see, I believe everything is connected. Every small, menial task that we do has a part in some grand outcome in our lives. So that's what I am going to do. I am going to recount everything in my life that I can remember and put it down in this book. If that seems boring to you, skip ahead to the parts you want to read. I mean it should be right there in the table of contents.

What part do you feel like reading? Drugs? My views on God and theology? An actual part about Tourette's?

Well they are ALL about Tourette's. That's what I'm trying to say about everything being connected. Every thought I have ever had, every action I have ever done, has been tied to my illness and my afflicted brain.

So let's being this story of my life.

And who knows? Maybe you'll learn something and this book won't be a waste of money.

AN ORIGIN STORY

I was born on June 6th 1993.

If you like numbers, here's a fun fact for you!

Take the month (6) the day (6) and subtract the last two digits of the year (9 - 3 = 6). You get 6/6/6.

Hey look at that!

I'm the devil.*

My uncle made that joke to my mother when she was pregnant with me.

She didn't appreciate that too much.

If you think that's just special, I also turned thirteen on June 6th 2006.

At 6:32

So if you remember that movie Jim Carrey was in where the number 23 was the bad guy, my birthdate and time contains both 666 and the number 23.

Aren't numbers fun?

She fell in love with the name ever since.

Kind of a weird way to acquire a name don't ya think?

My name is Tyler because my mother was watching television many decades ago and saw a dog food commercial where the dog was named Tyler.

---

* *Author's Note: I am actually not the devil. I cannot stress this enough.*

Anyway I lived in Bridgeview, Illinois for most of my baby years. I don't remember anything from that point in my life. Who does? I was a fucking baby, what do you want from me?

Later we moved to a town called Lockport. And that's where my first memory comes in.

My very first memory involves me, on a red tricycle. On top of a really big hill. Like from what I remember this hill was gigantic. Of course it wasn't. I visited that spot not too long ago, the 'hill' was more of a bump.

It's just that sometimes things we remember are a lot different from what actually happened. Things that seemed like huge difficulties in the past turn out to be minor inconveniences compared to what's coming down the road for us. Remember that. It'll be important later.

I've always been a weird kid. Ever since I was playing with plastic dinosaurs and watching Blue's Clues.

Let's start with my birth. That was weird enough.

I was an in vitro baby.

What does that mean exactly?

It means I was conceived in a petri dish instead of a womb.

My mother was having fertility issues and back in the 90's this hip, new way to have kids was all the rage.

I was one of eight fertilized eggs.

And I was the only one that survived.

That always resonated with me. Made me feel special. It's like I was the lone survivor.

I was also a very sick baby.

Apparently I would projectile vomit across the room.

Which is pretty damn impressive when you think about it.

I mean I was small, still kind of am (At the time of writing this I only weighed one hundred and fifty pounds) and I would vomit from one end of the room to another.

I probably resembled one of those water toys that you pinch and fill up with water, then squeeze and watch it shoot out.

Anyway I went to preschool a year late. I couldn't stand to be away from my mom. So started a legacy of always being the oldest one in class that would last until high school.

It's strange being the oldest and one of the smallest ones in class. Usually the kid whose held back is a brute and bigger and badder than everyone else. That's the trope anyway.

I don't know why I couldn't start school when I was supposed to.

As my parents would say I always went to the beat of my own drum. If I didn't feel like playing what all the other kids were playing, I'd sit and read a book.

I don't know what it was, I wasn't antisocial or anything, it was just that if you were playing something I didn't have any interest in, I would do something else.

Before showing any symptoms, I was a fairly miserable kid.

Of course, my OCD had a lot to do with that.

What's that? Oh ya, OCD is usually accompanied with Tourette's.

But more on that later, I'm trying to write a decent introduction here.

I've always been obsessed with death.

One time when I was six years old I started crying because I didn't want to die.

What kind of kid thinks like that?

Seriously that's fucked up.

Things didn't get truly crazy until I was diagnosed. That's where the real fun started. Of course, it took a while to get diagnosed because for a while my family and I had no idea what exactly was wrong with me.

ALL MY PROBLEMS

The first thing that happened was clearing my throat.

It really did feel like I had phlegm. A lot of it.

But of course that's what tics do to your brain. They make you think something is actually going on when there really isn't.

The coughing came next. And it really did feel like I couldn't breath.

Of course when this was going on my family just thought I had allergies and asthma.

I went through various treatments before we landed on Tourette's.

First we thought it was just plain old asthma.

I went through various inhalers and medications that probably fucked up my body worse than it already was.

I remember going to doctor after doctor to try to clear up the mysterious phlegm problem.

If only we had known what it was originally then this whole thing could have been avoided.

And I'd be a much happier kid.

But then I probably wouldn't have written this book so there ya go, let my suffering be the final piece of the puzzle to help someone else's kid and solve all their problems.

What a happy story for that kid.

Well I didn't have a book.

I didn't have a happy story.

I went through years of different meds and doctor visits and tons of money washed down the drain.

I remember getting acupuncture.

That actually didn't hurt that much.

In fact it sorta helped with stress.

Didn't solve the real problem.

Of my "Asthma"

But it certainly helped me relax.

If your tics aren't that bad I actually recommend it.

If they are that bad, please don't get it done.

You'll just end up stabbing yourself in a painful yet kind of funny-in-a-tragic-way experience.

I remember taking these god awful pills.

They tasted like death and vomit.

They were supposed to be all natural and holistic.

In fact we tried a lot of "all natural" remedies that ended up doing jack shit, and one that actually made the tics virtually disappear.

But I'll touch base on that in a little bit.

For awhile it seemed my too-early-too-officially-call-them-tics tics weren't that bad.

They were just so minor that we as a family didn't notice them.

That opens up a whole number of questions for many of you reading this book right now.

Do YOU have tics?

Even if you don't have Tourette's are you positive that you don't have any tics?

Like are your personality quirks just quirks or are they something else entirely?

Many people have tics and they aren't even aware of them.

Why am I saying this?

It's for you, the kid with the debilitating tics, to know that you aren't alone or even as much of a freak as you think.

You aren't alone.

Don't you ever forget that.

And you aren't a freak.

Don't ever forget that either.

Many people have what you have.

The CDC estimates that 3 in 1,000 children have Tourette's.

That doesn't seem like a lot?

That translates to over 148,000 children alone. Not counting adults.

But the CDC is unaware about how many people even have the disorder.

Like I said, sometimes it's so minor that you don't even notice.

So if that number (148,000) seems small, just remember that all that is, is 148,000 people just like you who knows exactly what you are going through.

148,000 people that share your experience.

148,000 people that have similar embarrassments and humiliations.

148,000 people that have expressed the same anger and frustration over their illness.

148,000 people.

So ya you're not alone.

It was my junior year of high school when I developed my more serious tics.

I remember the exact moment when I felt them.

I was playing *Fallout: New Vegas* when I felt a bizarre sensation in my left arm.

It felt like I needed to move it.

To twist and bend it.

Otherwise the feeling wouldn't go away.

Tics are an alien feeling to say the least.

They have no real purpose or reason behind them.

They just happen.

It's really hard to describe to people without tics.

You tic-less freaks.

Imagine a sort of pressure in an area.

It doesn't hurt, but you know it's just there.

It's always in the back of your mind.

You know you need to do something about it but you really don't know what.

What could you possibly do to make this sensation go away?

You can try moving the effected part.

Whether it be your arm, or your leg, or even your vocal cords.

You just need to express your body and try to shake off this sensation.

The feeling is, without a doubt, related to OCD.

OCD is a common tag-along illness for people with Tourette's.

Up to 60% of TS sufferers have been reported to have OCD symptoms. According to some medically sounding website.

And no you don't have OCD if you like your house to be clean.

Or I mean you could have OCD AND like your house to be clean but the two thing are not exactly related.

Most people think that OCD is just worrying about shit and cleaning feverishly.

They're wrong.

OCD is the nagging in your mind that you can't shake.

It's what makes people hoard old newspapers and junk "in case they need it"

It's what makes people turn around on the expressway and head home to make sure they locked the door.

OCD is a pretty serious thing.

It essentially controls every aspect of your life and can make you do some bizarre things.

When I was younger, I used to horde old magazines.

Why did I do this?

Because in my mind I thought it was possible for me to become stranded in my room, unable to get out due to some disaster or attack from aliens/robots/terrorists and I would need materials to start a fire with.

This is something I actually thought at one point.

The thing is even back then I knew that that was completely ridiculous.

That's perhaps the most interesting thing about OCD.

The people afflicted with it know that their rituals are ridiculous.

I know that my rituals were stupid and pointless yet I did them anyway.

Because they just felt right.

Here's a rundown of some of my OCD obsessions and compulsions:

- Checking locked doors
- Needing an even amount of things in my pockets
- Hoarding
- Constant worrying about everything. (Girls, Jobs, wondering if the food I just ate contains dairy, etc.)
- Checking my hair to see if it became uneven.
- Checking my face to see if it became uneven (seriously)
- Being unable to hold in fart. I needed that shit out of my body.
- Constantly thinking about the end of the world.
- Worrying about hurting people. Both emotionally and physically.
- Checking the bed and closet for serial killers.

I don't know if that last one is related to OCD or not but it's something weird that I used to do that I thought I should bring up.

I used to think that somehow a murderer would bypass our security system and locked doors and chose to hide under my bed or in my closet, waiting for me to go to sleep so they can murder my ass.

I'm not sure what checking would have done had there been a killer in my room.

It's not like once you find a murderer they just abandon their plans to kill you.

If anything it may have gotten me killed faster.

I realize that these things are silly and mentally draining yet I could not stop them for the life of me.

The only thing that has actually helped is medication.

I'll touch base on meds later.

But now I want to bring up two of my compulsions: Worrying that my face had become uneven and farting a lot.

Where does the OCD end and the tics begin?

That's what is so strange about the disorder. Is it indistinguishable from tics?

In order to "fix" my "uneven" face I would play with it.

Adjusting my face and sometimes even hitting it.

It felt like my jaw was longer on one side compared to the other.

That my eyes were different sizes.

That was nose moved around.

I am obsessed with my face.

I don't know if it's because I am devilishly handsome or not.

If, god forbid, I get a pimple, I must remove it immediately.

I can't stand to have something on my face be it a pus filled bump or a scab or a stray strand of hair that grew in the middle of my cheek for some reason.

I feel like once it's there it's the most noticeable thing on my face.

That everyone is looking at me.

Judging me.

Obviously this isn't true, and part of me knew this.

But it couldn't be stopped.

I couldn't shake the feeling of imperfection.

I personally believe this to be a huge part of OCD and Tourette's.

Perfection and Imperfection.

People with tics want to reach this perfect equilibrium between tics.

This perfect state where the sensation is gone.

When that sensation is there it is an imperfection in the afflicted body part.

Your leg just doesn't feel right, so you should shake it.

Your arm is tingling so you should bend it.

Your throat is itchy so you should clear it as loud as possible.

The same goes for OCD.

You need to check if that door is locked.

Because if it isn't locked it's imperfect.

And when things are imperfect bad things are allowed to happen.

Someone could break into your house if that door is unlocked.

Your kids might really be in danger if you don't call them.

Your face might really be uneven, and then you're ugly.

No one wants to be ugly.

Things need to be perfect for those with OCD.

If you think about it from an evolutionary stand point, it makes sense.

Think about cavemen for a bit.

Imagine the hairy, jacked, loin-clothed individual hunting wooly mammoths and gathering berries in the forest.

Think about how he lived.

Now imagine he has OCD.

What would that be like?

We think of mental disorders as recent events, that they didn't exist tens of thousands of years ago.

Wouldn't being obsessed with perfection actually be an advantage back then?

Think about it: The caveman obsessed with keeping his cave the cleanest probably would never die of infection.

The cavewoman who always had to know where her children were most likely prevented them from dying a few times, letting them carry on and reproduce, furthering the blood line.

The caveman who kept his berry stockpile in perfect condition and away from bugs had enough to eat during the winter.

This is all speculation.

I am not an expert in any way.

I said that at the beginning of this book.

Haven't you been paying attention?

But you, the humble book reader, most admit it makes sense.

But I'm getting ahead of myself.

I'll talk about all that stuff later when I've run out of things to write about and need to fill up some more pages.

Anyway let's get back on track.

OCD?

Ya, OCD.

In case you think you have OCD, that depends on what your obsessions and compulsions are.

Do you like having clean hands?

Maybe you wash them a lot?

That's not having OCD, that's called not being a fucking pig.

You should like having clean hands and you should clean them a lot.

Doesn't mean you automatically have OCD.

That's possibly one of the most annoying things about having OCD.

Listen to other people talk about how they also have "OCD".

Most people have personality quirks.

You can be a worrier, doesn't mean you have OCD.

It just means that you're paranoid.

It's only when it interferes with your daily life.

When you can barely function in the real world, then it's OCD.

If you're just uncomfortable when someone grabs a doorknob before you do and you think it's dirty now, that's not having OCD.

You're just a prissy pants.

I want to bring up one of my obsessions here.

The one where I worry about hurting people.

It's a strange obsession because it feels like part of me wants to hurt people.

Sitting in the doctors office, listening to what they have to say what's wrong of me.

So I day dream.

Sometimes I day dream about punching him right in the face.

I like my doctor too and I would never do this.

But the feeling can't be shaked.

It's not just physical pain either.

One time I was leaving a creative writing class during my second year of college when I started having a conversation with two of my classmates.

We had this random heart-to-heart moment where we talked about our lives and our dreams and our hopes.

It was truly beautiful.

So naturally my brain started making me think of ways to ruin it.

One of my classmates was an older woman.

Must have been late forties early fifties.

Anyway she had two children, two daughters, who are handicapped.

One had spina bifida and autism.

I forgot what the other daughter had.

The point is when she told me this, I couldn't stop thinking of the word "retard".

I was constantly thinking about it during our conversation.

To the point where it got distracting.

I couldn't stop thinking about it.

"What if I said it?" was the main thought racing through my mind.

Scenarios were I did say it played like movies in my head.

I was obsessed with thinking about ruining this poor woman's day.

I knew if I did say "retard" it would devastate her.

That's why I was obsessed with it.

I have a friend with a mentally handicapped brother and that same thought plays in my head whenever he's around.

I don't know why I think about hurting people all the time.

I know violent thoughts are common with OCD.

Does that scare you?

Do I sound dangerous?

Do I sound like a freak?

It's ok, like I said earlier I know it's messed up.

I know these persistent thoughts are silly and unwanted by myself and society.

I know right from wrong.

I never try to intentionally hurt someone even though sometimes that's all I can think about.

There is a disorder called OCPD, obsessive compulsive personality disorder, where the afflicted cannot tell that their obsessions and compulsions are stupid and unimportant.

They really think they do something.

Can you imagine having that?

Doing so many silly things and thinking that they actually mattered?

Then again who says that doesn't happen to all of us right now?

Everyone has obsessions and rituals and quirks.

OCD or not.

We go through our lives doing so many little pointless things and we think they actually matter in the grand scheme of the universe.

We think getting rejected by the cute classmate actually matters.

We think having a shitty summer job actually affects us and who we are in some way.

We think messing up and making mistakes have some sort of outcome that we will truly remember in our long lives.

Truth is most things don't matter.

That's really the only tip I can give you if you're like me.

OCD.

Tourette's.

Some other problem you have.

The shit we do in our day to day lives really doesn't matter.

That may sound like the most depressing news ever but in reality it should be the best news you've heard all day.

Most things you do don't matter.

That's fantastic news!

Now you can stop worrying so much about every little thing.

Think about what really matters in life.

- Food and water.
- Shelter and Security
- Family (not just blood related) and friends.
- What you did with your life before you died.

Everything else is unimportant shit that we put on some pedestal and keep at the peak of our interests.

Getting rejected by someone.

Being bored for a few hours.

Forgetting to record a show you like.

None of that shit matters in the long run.

That's really the best way to overcome any problem.

Think about how pointless it is.

There's a real beauty in it.

Trust me.

Life is better when you realize that most things that most people do and say have no impact on how your life will turn out.

If someone gets mad at you for not liking their oh-so-hilarious Facebook status, why do you care?

Someone you know is rude to you? Maybe they're having a bad day and made the wrong choice, or maybe they are just a toxic person. If the former is true, they will apologize later. If they don't or the truly are a toxic person, then why would you want to continue to associate with them? Why would you want them to like you?

Of course it took me awhile to get on that path.

For a while I cared a lot about everything.

Every little thing.

Having tics doesn't make it any easier.

Every stare.

Every laugh you hear behind your back.

Every dumbass question of "Are you okay?"

It really does get to you at a point.

And for the longest time I really did care about all of that.

I didn't see the pointlessness.

All I saw was my life turning upside down.

Funny thing about your whole life changing in a week's notice.

You tend to get depressed.

My depression started with the onset of my tics.

And it stayed with me for years.

What really makes you depressed is when you think you're on the path to a cure and it just falls through your hands.

When you think that you have something and in the end it turns to nothing.

You wanna know how many times that has happened to me?

To just have the rug pulled out from under you?

There was one time in the beginning of this whole mess that is my life where we thought we had the answer.

Back when we thought this was related to allergies.

Back when my only problem was clearing my throat.

I used to spit a lot too.

That was one of the most disgusting and disturbing tics.

To just spit everywhere.

Like in my own fucking house.

On the carpet.

I would spit everywhere.

Sometimes on my own shoes.

I'd carry around empty water bottles and spit it them like I was chewing tobacco.

This was before we knew what was wrong with me so naturally my family just assumed I had a lot of phlegm and bad manners.

We saw a lot of allergists back in the day.

I also had trouble breathing.

Or at least it seemed like I had trouble breathing.

I remember the feeling, it was like I didn't have enough air.

Was that actually a tic?

Who can tell?

All I know is that it certainly didn't seem normal at the time.

We all assumed I had asthma.

There was a lot of assuming going on back then.

I'm not sure if people wanted to admit that it was Tourette's back then.

One doctor said it was all in my head.

We never went back to him.

We were angry.

We didn't dare think this was mental or neurological.

We didn't dare admit I wasn't perfect.

That was the main problem back then.

No one wanted to come out and say "Tourette's"

Because that's a big, scary word that would mean I was mentally handicapped right?

Wrong, of course but there is a stigma that is associated with neurological problems.

And that's because there is a stigma with mental problems.

See, people confuse the two.

We as a society group them together like they're the same thing.

But really they are completely different.

Neurological illnesses deal with the nervous system, they have nothing to do with your state of mind.

I'm not "crazy".

I do not have a mental illness (Well I do have OCD…)

However stress does have a huge factor in neurological disorders.

Whenever I get stressed my tics go haywire.

And I'm certain if you have Tourette's you can agree.

When I was picking my classes for college I flipped shit.

When I had a big test in high school I used to distract everyone in class.

Probably wasn't anybody's favorite student. Or classmate.

I'll talk about school in a later chapter.

There is enough there to write a whole other book now that I think about it.

Anyway back to my tics-before-we-knew-they-were-tics tics.

So ya I spit and coughed a lot for no reason.

It was a pretty disgusting habit I'll admit.

One that I wasn't necessarily proud of.

What did we do about these problems?

Cut out part of my esophagus of course!

I had an endoscopy to alleviate my "acid reflux".

A little biopsy to ride myself of the spitting and coughing up all that phlegm.

I remember the procedure pretty well.

I woke up early to go to the hospital.

I remember getting the IV to knock myself out cold.

When I woke up I had a terrible pain in my nose that caused me to tear up immediately.

I had three feet of packing in my nasal cavity.

You know that scene in *Iron Man* when he gets knocked out with his own bomb and wakes up in the terrorist's cave and pulls that stuff out of his nose?

Pretty gross scene.

You know what scene I'm talking about right?

That was me.

Circa 2006.

Of course it was a lot worse.

Or at least it seemed worse than how the movie portrayed.

Seriously, imagine having three feet of packing tissue in your nasal cavity.

Then imagine having it pulled out sloooowly.

I remembered a *Scooby-Doo* movie was on in the hospital room.

Something about witches and warlocks.

I wasn't really paying attention.

Well, cause I HAD THREE FEET OF TISSUE PAPER STUFFED UP MY NOSE.

That's not a common thing that people have done.

And it was all in the name of stopping a thing that we didn't even realize was purely neurological at the time.

How were we supposed to know that these were tics at the time?

How were we supposed to come to the conclusion that I was "messed up"?

I mean having Tourette's has a stigma to it.

That you're crazy or retarded.

And I don't need to tell you that that is a bunch of bullshit.

We are not crazy.

Not that I'm saying its bad thing, but we aren't retarded either.

We are just kids with a confusing illness and nowhere else to turn.

Family and Friends help.

If you only have one of those, be thankful you have at least one.

If you don't have either, well then you're partly to blame.

Go get some friends.

Don't let an illness set you back socially.

(More on that later on in the book)

Anyway after that endoscopy, nothing much changed.

I still spat everywhere.

My breathing was better however.

I will admit that.

So maybe there was an actual problem there that was just a coincidence.

Eventually I stopped spitting everywhere.

I did keep clearing my throat however.

That was the "change".

I should probably elaborate.

Tics change.

One month you could be flailing your arms around like an idiot.

The next you could be screeching at the top of your lungs or nodding your head like your saying "yes" to an unknown series of questions.

My tics changed a lot over the years.

Let me list all the ones I have ever had:

- Coughing
- Clearing my throat
- Yelling
- Cracking my knuckles
- Shaking my legs
- Shaking my head
- Shaking my arms
- Twitching
- Spitting
- Smelling my fingers (yes that's a real tic)
- Anal tics (farting and/or sharting)
- Double-stepping (like a double take with your foot)
- Grunting
- Grinding my teeth
- Punching myself in various body parts (yes that means the penis)
- Twisting and squeezing whatever is in my hand (yes this also means the penis)

These are the tics I have had (or currently have).

Some have come and gone. Never to be felt again.

Others come and go whenever they please.

I mentioned before how alien the feeling of a tic can be.

I didn't mention how peculiar it is when one goes away however.

It really is just a change overnight.

One day you're flapping your arms like a chicken, the next morning your lower back feels like it needs to be cracked so you gyrate your torso in a really weird way.

And it stays like that for months, possibly years.

Then one morning your back spasm is gone and now you're twisting your neck around like your trying out for the new *Exorcist* movie.

Tics are a strange occurrence.

One that I do not have the qualifications nor the legitimate research available to give an exact answer to why they happen.

All I know is that "Shit happens"

That's the great life lesson I've learned over the years.

That saying has been my therapist throughout my diagnosis.

My life coach.

My simple blessing.

This sounds really pessimistic and depressing but in reality it's not so bad.

If anything it's hardened me to withstand more challenging obstacles in my life.

Shit happens.

Shit happened in November 2011 when I was sitting in my basement playing *Fallout: New Vegas*.

When my arm felt a little funny.

When as the days went by my neck started hurting and the only way to relieve the pain and sensation was to head bang like I was at a heavy metal concert.

It was when my dad saw me one day in the home office, that's when the fun started.

When the misdiagnosis and the false diseases and the fear of the unknown began.

Of course he didn't know what the hell was wrong with me.

He was just concerned like any parent would be.

So naturally we thought of some pretty fucking stupid treatments.

I have really sweaty hands.

That's important to this story actually.

I was doing this home remedy for sweaty hands.

It's where you put your hands in water filled pans with an electric charge running through them.

Does that make any sense at all?

Of course not.

But when you're desperate for a solution, anything makes sense.

So naturally when I started moving around in a strange fashion we naturally thought that the sweaty hands treatment had something to do with.

Like I was being electrocuted or some bullshit.

I don't know, but that theory didn't last too long for obvious reasons.

It was when we saw an actual doctor when we got my diagnosis.

But it really didn't make sense at the time.

Because how could I have Tourette's?

Neither of me parents did.

And I wasn't born with it, my symptoms started up when I was seventeen, really like twelve if you count my early tics like throat clearing.

The doctor prescribed me a drug called Topamax.

Which is a medication for epilepsy.

Why was I given it?

Who the hell knows!

All I know is that it worked really well for about a month, then caused me to have even more violent tics.

This was the point where I was yelling.

Like screeching at the top of my lungs.

I couldn't go out anywhere. And this was in the summer time.

So I was a hermit for a while.

I got acquainted with Netflix during that phase.

So I mean … silver linings and what not.

School was out so that was a plus.

At least my tics had the courtesy to get really bad AFTER my social life (what little remained anyway) wasn't at risk.

They went from "Pretty noticeable" to "Holy hell what is wrong with that kid!?"

So we stopped taking the Topamax.

Obviously.

Then something (unfortunate and) interesting happened.

One day I was sitting at the computer, eating a plum, when my mother noticed something.

It was around noon when I started having tics.

I was decent all morning.

Up until I ate that plum.

Was plums the secret answer to Tourette's?

Just stop eating plums and you'll never tic again?

No.

But maybe foods high in sugar was the key.

So I stopped eating candy and fruit for a bit. Just to see if that was true.

My tics were certainly better.

We also cut caffeine and any "energy producing foods and beverages" from my diet.

Things were going pretty well but I was still bad tic-wise.

So things got a little desperate.

We cut out ALL sugar.

Like even natural.

Dextrose.

Maltose.

Sucrose.

All the oses.

Is that healthy?

Of course not.

But we were desperate.

I say this because I want to teach you something very valuable: Just because something makes you feel better, doesn't mean it's a good thing.

We'll get more in depth on that when I talk about medication side effects.

But anyway back to this insane diet I was on.

This may seem like a good idea to any desperate parents out there looking for a solution or any source of relief.

But it's a bad idea.

I did a gluten-free, dairy-free, sugar –free, and carb-free diet.

We realized that since carbs breakdown into glucose, a type of sugar, that carbs made me tic more often.

The only problem is when you stop eating all those foods, you tend to lose a lot of weight.

And losing all that weight in a short amount of time isn't exactly healthy.

By which I mean that it's not at all healthy.

I'm no doctor but I do think that an eighteen year old shouldn't weigh one hundred and twenty pounds.

The worst thing about it was that it didn't even stop all my tics.

I was still pretty bad.

And also school lunches were a bitch to pack.

Can't eat the cafeteria food, can't eat bread.

What the hell can I eat?

Organic meats and lettuce wrapped in a corn tortilla.

That's what I ate for school for the better half of a year.

That and like random tasteless crackers for a side dish.

That doesn't sound like a bad lunch really.

I'm not trying to sounds picky.

But the same thing for five days week, for about eight months.

Not only does that start to suck after the hundredth time, but it also burns a hole in your wallet as well.

Eating all organic and vegan and gluten free foods costs a lot of money.

But like I said before, desperate times call for desperate measures.

We were just looking for a solution to a problem we didn't understand.

And how could we understand?

The doctor we first went to didn't do anything except tell us what was wrong with me, he didn't say anything like "Here's how to combat the symptoms".

He just flat out told us that there is nothing we can do.

Can you imagine how that felt?

You wake up one day with a problem and then somebody tells you that you'll never be normal again.

It was infuriating, depressing, and a little humbling all at the same time.

Why was it humbling?

Imagine thinking you're at the top of the world.

Nothing can bring you down.

You were born for a reason and God loves you and has a plan for you.

You're the future savior of humanity and you're perfect in every way.

Then one day you're told you're not perfect.

That you're flawed.

Maybe you're not born for a reason.

Maybe you're not the future savior of humanity.

God doesn't love you and there is no plan.

I'd love to get into my pessimistic views on life but I'll save that for a different chapter.

This chapter is about all the weird shit I tried in attempt to "cure" myself.

Me and my family's dilemmas in attempt to play God and treat a disease that is mysterious still unknown to many.

Want to hear another thing we did?

We thought that a nerve in my jaw was causing the tics.

Does that make any sense?

It does when you're looking for answers.

There was a doctor in Washington D.C that was promising a cure for tics.

It was a mouth piece.

That was the miracle cure.

A mouth piece.

His logic was that there is a nerve in your jaw that was being aggravated by your jawbone.

This nerve was responsible for movement.

And when this nerve is being pushed on by your jawbone, tics form.

It's a little hard to swallow but at the time it made perfect sense to us.

It made sense because I had a problem with my jaw called TMJ dysfunction which stand for Temporomandibular joint.

I complained my jaw hurt a lot and I would stretch it and move my jaw around.

Of course this was probably just a tic.

But at the time we didn't really know what a tic was and what was something else.

We were new to this.

No one in my family never really dealt with anything like this before.

So we did what any desperate and in the dark person would do.

We went to Washington D.C.

It was just me and my dad on a road trip.

We left our home around five thirty in the morning.

I slept in the car.

When I woke up we were already in Indiana.

We had a long trip ahead of us.

I had never been on such a long drive before.

The farthest we have ever driven before was Ohio.

And when we passed Toledo, Ohio. Well, that was a completely undiscovered territory for me.

Like a whole new country.

We got to Pennsylvania when we hit a traffic jam.

We stayed in there for hours, not knowing just what the hell caused this pile up to begin with.

I was curious (and bored) so I got out of the car and left.

I walked for a good fifteen minutes when I saw what was causing the pile up.

A Hostess truck had turned on its side.

I got there just in time to see them try to lift up the truck.

And when they did, hundreds of Twinkies just fall out of this giant hole in the side of the truck.

What does that have to do with anything?

Absolutely nothing I just thought it was cool.

That trip was pretty interesting though.

I mean it was a good excuse to go to our nation's capital.

We went to the Smithsonian too.

The security guard thought he was fucking hilarious by imitating one of my tics.

I ignored him the best I could.

I wanted to say: "Fuck you" but in all probability he didn't know what was wrong with me, but still, imitating people is childish, you're a grown ass man, what the hell is wrong with you?

Anyway it was a cool museum.

If you haven't gone, I highly recommend.

So we get to the doctor's office.

And he starts of his little speech about how my nerves in my jaw are causing tics.

And he shows us these video he made, little before and after clips of former patients.

The thing is, these people are actually doing great.

He shows his mouthpiece.

A strange looking device that looked like your standard retainer except for it being about ten times taller.

It fit poorly in my mouth.

Stretching it to its limit.

I sit there in his office with my mouth full of ceramic and metal.

Nearly tic free.

I'm amazed that I could sit still for so long.

Mind you that this was during a horrible period when I was twisting and shouting non-stop.

Tears almost run down my face as I sit in the office.

But I hold them in.

I'm with my dad.

And I'm not a pussy.

I am amazed about how my tics just stopped?

Could this be it?

Could this be the end of an shitty, shitty era?

Is this too good to be true?

Of course it is.

We left the doctor's office with our heads held high.

"This might work" we thought.

He gave us a make-shift retainer made up of popsicle sticks and rubber bands.

The next step was getting a MRI to view my jaw. So they can build a my very own retainer that fit me perfectly.

The doctor says to me: "We know you have a ... condition. Can you sit still long enough?"

I loved how he danced around eggshells asking me if this whole thing is a waste of time or not.

We began the procedure and as you'd expect it didn't work out so well.

The doctors recommend that I listen to music to help calm myself down.

They gave me headphones and I put them on and got back in the tube of the MRI machine.

It was Creed playing.

I had to lay in the machine, putting Popsicle sticks in my mouth to stretch it so they could take better pictures.

The weird thing is, the more Popsicle sticks in my mouth, the more relief I felt.

Maybe there is some science to what this doctor is saying.

After the results were sent to the main doctor, he started making the retainer.

I got my very own the next day.

It barely fit in my mouth, just like the last time, despite this one being designed solely for that purpose.

I wore it thought.

I hated it already but I wore it because it gave me some relief.

I still had tics they were just suppressed.

We still had some time to kill and hey, we were in Washington D.C. Might as well enjoy ourselves for a bit.

We went to the movies.

We saw *Green Lantern.*

I don't know if you remember that movie, but it wasn't really worth remembering now was it?

We sat through the movie in silence. Something that was a rarity for me.

I remember the way my mouth was distorted, it looked like I was constantly saying "Oh".

I would shove pretzel rods through the hole that my mouth my making and suck the salt off.

Sounds gross?

In hindsight, it probably wasn't the most courteous thing to do in a movie theater.

But hey, better than shouting at the top of your lungs.

We began the drive back.

It was a completely different car ride.

On the way there I was yelling and moving around like a possessed man.

On the way back I was relatively calm.

When we got home my family thought this was the first step toward a cure.

The only problem was I was only good when the mouthpiece stayed in, and when it was in I was limited per say.

I couldn't talk, or eat.

Laying down on my side wasn't an option.

And whenever I slept it would fall out during the night.

We heard about one mother who had it glued to her son's bottom teeth.

He was a swimmer and it kept falling out in the pool.

We opted not to go that extreme, especially when it stopped working.

I started having the same amount of tics with or without the mouth piece.

The weird thing was that the make-shift retainer made up of Popsicle sticks worked better than the actual mouthpiece.

But it's not like I could walk around with wooden sticks in my mouth all day.

I kept on wearing the original mouthpiece, despite it losing its effectiveness.

Did it work?

Kinda. It worked for a little while but ultimately it failed.

Does that mean it won't work for you?

Of course not, it seems like it worked great for some people.

Was it worth $5000?

Of course not. That's a ludicrous price for something that is sketchy science at best.

We got tired of waiting for this miraculous device to work so we stopped.

And I went back on that wonderful diet.

Which I cannot stress enough, is a terrible idea.

Once I hit one hundred and twenty pounds, we knew we should stop the diet.

It was just too risky and unhealthy.

I would still have to avoid really sugary foods, but other than that we decided that I should eat normally.

We tried neuro-feedback once.

It worked pretty well but not well enough for the cost.

They glued wires to my head and I watch a movie about bicycle racing.

I don't know what it was called and I don't know where to start to even look for something like that.

Actually hold on ....

Holy shit I found it!

It was called *Breaking Away* and it was about this kid who liked to speak Italian and ride bicycles entered some kind of race.

It was called *Breaking Away* and it was about this kid who liked to speak Italian and ride bicycles entered some kind of race.

I don't know there was a college involved. He was a high school kid posing as a college kid or something.

I don't really feel like doing any research to find out more about the movie.

I mean I guess I could just go on Wikipedia and look up the plot synopsis but I don't feel like doing that.

I like my description better.

Kid who rides bicycles and speaks Italian grows up in home town and enters a race or something.

I never did finish that movie, the sessions were too expensive.

Anyway they hooked up wires to my brain and we watched the movie.

Whenever my brain went out of focus or something, the screen turned grey.

I forgot the doctors exact words but it was something like my brain my readjusting itself.

Did it help?

Not really.

It did improve my mood however.

It made me less irritable and less angry.

I actually enjoyed being around me family.

We also tried what's called a "hyperbaric chamber"

It was a six foot long, one foot wide tube that you lay in.

The idea is that you're breathing in pure oxygen and that increases the amount of oxygen in your red blood cells.

I wrote this in 2014, it is currently 2019 and I have still not finished that movie.

Did it work?

No, but I felt fucking jacked afterwards.

Seriously sometimes I'd go workout right afterwards because I felt so energized.

Once again though it wasn't really worth the money.

We just tried whatever sounded somewhat legitimate.

There was another thing we tried.

Something that no one really knows if it's legitimate or not.

It's debated among the scientific community and I can see both sides.

I got really depressed during my senior year of high school.

It's not like I wasn't used to my tics by then, I was.

It was because for a while, I thought my family and I had thought we had found a cure.

Sounds too good to be true?

Maybe it was, but what we found unlocked a new path that we went down.

Pandas.

Not the cute Asian bear.

PANDAS.

Pediatric Autoimmune Neuropsychiatric Disorders Associated with Streptococcal infections.

Really it should be PANDASI but whatever PANDAS sounds adorable.

It's really anything but however.

The theory goes that the streptococcus bacteria that causes strep throat goes a little haywire and infiltrates your body.

From there the bacterium supposedly mimics your nerve endings, tricking your immune cells to target your nerves.

That causes tics.

The thing is the strep dies pretty quickly once you start taking antibiotics.

Yet your immune system still targets your cells.

Does that make sense?

I still don't know.

They say that PANDAS effects children and by the time we found it I was 18.

But I also have a baby face so maybe I just age slower than normal.

We saw a doctor who specialized in PANDAS.

We saw him and he seemed like he knew what he was talking about.

The only thing was he charged $500 a visit.

He offered a procedure that was $30,000.

Part of me wondered if he really cared at all and was just interested in the money.

We got to the hospital and they hooked me up to an IV.

The procedure was called IVIG or intravenous immunoglobulin.

The idea was that my antibodies were causing my tics, so if we overloaded my system with antibodies then my body would shut down production of them. After a while, my body would resume making normal antibodies again that wouldn't attack my nervous system.

Does that make sense?

I don't know I'm not a doctor.

They hooked me up to the IV stand and put the Immunoglobulin in me.

I remember laying next to a little girl who was mute.

Evidently she had PANDAS too but it manifested differently.

Does THAT make sense? I'll tell you one thing though: It worked . . . .

. . . for about two weeks.

Yep, I was tic free for fourteen whole days.

And it was lovely.

Unfortunately those fourteen days weren't eternity.

And eventually I was back to square one.

I was, however, a little better than I was before.

I could hold tic in for longer periods of time.

And my tic were less severe afterwards.

So did it work?

Kind of.

Maybe there is something to PANDAS that we just don't understand.

It's why doctors in some of the most prestigious schools and hospitals are doing tests right now to try to figure out what would work in treating this disease.

Since it worked for a little while the first time, my family decided to try it a second time.

This of course set us back another $30,000.

And the second time the nurse forgot to give me a heated blanket.

Is that a big deal?

I didn't think so.

Until my body temperature dropped and I started shaking uncontrollably.

I was shivering so intensely that I projectile vomited all over my mother.

I laid in bed for hours after puking.

I felt like I was hit by a truck.

I still have no idea why I got so sick.

Was the medicine too cold?

Could that really do something to a person?

Make them shake like that?

I don't know but I certainly didn't want to try the IVIG a third time.

After that we kind of ran out of ideas.

My mom found something online that was supposed to help kids with violent tics.

It was quite the unlikely source however.

It was camel milk.

Yep. Camel milk.

Evidently the people selling it were claiming that it was like a little IVIG treatment in a bottle.

We ordered it.

Setting us back about $500 each time we did.

And I tried some good old fashioned camel juice.

It was surprisingly good.

I am allergic to cow's milk so I hadn't had milk of any animal origin in a while.

It was actually quite delicious.

Weird as hell but tasty.

Plus as an added bonus, it seemed to suppress my tics to a pretty good degree.

I have no idea about the science behind it.

Maybe it really is like a little IVIG in a bottle.

But would that mean PANDAS is a correct diagnosis?

Once again, I have no idea.

What I do know is that I drank two bottles every day until it seemed to lose its effectiveness.

Maybe the whole thing was mental and I was just wishing it to work so it seemed to work.

Mind over matter sort of thing.

I would drink a bottle before I went to school and it would tide me over for a few hours.

Just a little relief so I didn't embarrass myself too badly in front on everyone in class.

It just got too expensive to keep doing however.

We didn't have $500 a month to spend on milk.

It became too ridiculous.

What we needed was a cheap, easy to get alternative tic suppressor.

That's the line of thinking that lead my dad to buy me marijuana.

What's that you ask?

Illegal to say?

Of course it was.

But here's the thing: it wasn't high in THC. (The main ingredient in marijuana that gets you high.)

It was high in CBD.

CBD is the only molecule contained in weed that has shown quite some promise in the medical field.

It all started when we were watching the news, and there was a report out of Colorado (the first state to legalize recreational marijuana in case you've been living under a rock for the past few years)

Apparently people with epilepsy were using a strain of weed to cope with their seizures.

My dad thought that since it helped with epilepsy, maybe it would help with Tourette's.

Does that make sense?

Who gives a shit my parents were going to get me weed, and I wouldn't have to pay for it.

It was the dream come true.

My dad got the stuff, I still don't know how (because I never asked. Once again, who cares? Free weed!)

And every now and then I would smoke in my garage.

My parents wanted to hide what they were doing to my little sisters, because lecturing them on drugs and why their big brother was taking them all the time didn't seem like a fun, family event.

So there I was, lighting up in the garage every time my tics got really bad.

It was fun, not going to lie. (why would I lie now? I've been brutally honest this entire book so far.)

My dad rolled some pretty nice joints despite being so against pot.

I would smoke in my car and listen to the radio.

See, unbeknownst to my parents: this CBD weed was also very high in THC as well.

Well I am also a lightweight, but you get the picture.

So while I would sit in my car and listen to the radio, I would trip major balls.

One time I listened to the entire album of Pink Floyd's *Dark Side of the Moon* in my bedroom with lights off, with a bag of chips for company.

If you had never gotten high and listen to that album in dark while eating snacks, you sir, or madam, are missing out.

So did it work?

Of course it did.

I highly recommend medical marijuana to suppress your tics.

Whether you get it legitimately or not.

Just be careful not to get caught by the fuzz.

And please smoke responsibly.

In the upcoming chapter I discuss all about relying on substances for relief.

Don't do it.

Don't overindulge.

Don't be one of those people who depend of something to get by with their daily lives.

Of course I couldn't rely on weed to get me better.

So we made an appointment with a neurologist in Chicago to see if we could a get a more permanent solution.

We heard of something called DBS or, Deep Brain Stimulation, and wanted a piece of that action.

DBS is where they put electrodes in a specific spot in your brain.

Which spot?

Well it's different for everybody.

And they stimulate this spot with constant electricity.

This way the area of your brain producing tics is never triggered to make any more tics.

Does it work?

Well the thing is I never got it done.

When we saw this neurologist we brought this up immediately.

I didn't want to spend the rest of my life on pills.

Plus we tried pills before (remember how the Topamax turned out?)

He insisted we try more pills first.

Why?

Well because having brain surgery is something the medical field calls "Risky and fucking terrifying"

It's not a guaranteed cure-all like we believed.

That spot in the brain that's different for everyone?

That's called the nucleus.

And like I said, everyone's is different.

Because of that, they have to do this surgery *while your awake* so you can tell them what "feels right" in regards to where your brain is being poked and zapped.

I've read a lot of stories about people with Tourette's who have this procedure done.

Sometimes it works sometimes it doesn't.

What I do know is that it's reserved for people with severe tics and people who couldn't tolerate medications.

(I actually talk to a girl who had this procedure done. Read about it in the chapter "Kayley's Story")

So we tried a new medication first.

I am currently on what's called Orap, or Pimozide.

Does it work?

It does for me.

I feel great actually.

I still have tics.

But they are mostly under control.

I can now sit still in a movie theater and keep quiet during the good parts.

I can finally play hide and seek and not be the first one found.

Is Orap for everybody?

No.

Well maybe.

Tourette's is a tricky disease.

Not every medication is going to work for everybody.

Some work for some people, some make you tic more if you have a bad reaction to it.

It's like playing Russian roulette but instead of being shot, you have a terrible reaction to a medication that puts you in the hospital. (Seriously make sure you read "Kayley's story". Scary shit in that chapter)

What works for me may not work for you.

The point I'm trying to make is see a professional who knows what he or she is talking about.

See someone who you can trust and one that actually cares about your well-being.

If you have Tourettes, skip all the other stuff and just go see a neurologist.

They know what they are talking about.

After all their whole career is based on the nervous system.

If you have a disease where your nervous system is acting up, who do you think you should go see?

If you are a worried individual who doesn't understand what' happening to their bodies, or are a worried parent who can't seem to help their child, this is the right next step.

These medications were designed by professionals to help other people.

The side effects are scary, but it's worth it in order to find the right medication.

You might not react nicely to any medication, well that's where the DBS comes in.

It's the only way to know to if you need it.

Trust your doctor.

They want to help.

Well that's about it.

Everything I have tried in a desperate attempt to cure myself.

Of course I realize now that there is not cure, only treatments.

Tourette's is something you will learn to deal with.

You really have no other option.

Killing yourself isn't a solution. (Seriously do not do that. Please)

It's something that you just have to get used to, just like the people around you if they are displeased with your condition, will have to get used to you.

Things will get better.

I promise.

One day you will meet people who don't give a shit whether you have tics or not.

Maybe you already met those people and just didn't realize it.

I don't know you story.

But now you know mine.

Or at least part of mine.

There's still a lot of pages left I guess.

That was kind of a stupid thing to say.

I'm sorry.

But anyway like I said, things will get better.

I promise.

BEN'S STORY

Let's take a break from myself.

What do I mean?

I mean let us see another story.

Another viewpoint.

You didn't think I was going to talk about myself for however many pages did you?

How conceded do you think I am?

While that article I mentioned for *Cracked.com* I met two individuals with Tourette's as well.

(Obviously they had Tourette's since they contributed to the article about Tourette's.)

I contacted both of my co-writers and asked if they would be so kind to do an interview with me for this very book.

They agreed.

And without further ado I will introduce you to two more kids with the same symptoms as me.

The same symptoms as you.

Benjamin was born in 1991.

At the time of me writing this he was 23.

He lives in Cape Cod, Massachusetts.

Ben was first diagnosed at age six.
I asked him about his tics to break the ice.

Me: So tell me about the kind of tics you've had over the years.

Ben: First they were simple tics. Eye blinking, nose twitching. Then at thirteen I started barking. I work at a restaurant now and people ask "Is there a dog in the back?" sometimes. Then my senior year of high school I started having vocal tics.

Me: Damn. Like saying words and phrases?

Ben: Exactly. Really weird shit too. Like one time that's famous with my friends is me saying "Butterscotch dinosaur pussy".

Me: ... you're shitting me (Laughs).

Ben: Yep haha.

Me: Butterscotch dinosaur pussy.

Ben: ya I say weird sentences sometimes. Occasionally it'll seem like I'm speaking in tongues too. I've been told it looks like straight out of a demonic possession movies.

Me: God those movies suck. Anyway that's not the point. What kind of things would you say?

Ben: Like, for example, we had German exchange students at my school. They actually thought I was trying to speak to them.

Me: I see. What kind of medication are you on? If that is, you take it at all.

Ben: I am on this stuff called Geodon. But that's for my Bipolar. Not my tics.

Me: Oh you're bipolar as well. You really got the shit end of the stick.

Ben: Yep (laughs) I also have ADHA but I can't mix my Tourette's medication with it so I basically have to choose between having tics and paying attention.

Me: Kind of how I have to make a choice. Have tics or have my dick work.

Ben: (Laughs) What?!

Me: Oh my medication causes erectile dysfunction.

Ben: Ah I see. Well that sucks.

Me: Ya but hey it's not like I'm getting any action anyway. Let's talk more about you. Have you tried anything else to get rid of your tics?

Ben: Ya I was going to be part of a study for DBS but it seemed a little scary.

Me: Well ya it's brain surgery. It IS scary.

Ben: My neurologist is Dr. Jeremiah Scharf. Google him and you'll get a lot of results

(I did and he is quite famous in his field)

Ben: He is currently doing a study looking at the cellular level of Tourette's.

Me: Care to elaborate? This seems really interesting.

Ben: Well there was research that he was a part of, looking at the genes of people with Tourette's. He found a rare mutation in them. The gene mutated was involved in the histamine system of the brain. Mice with lower brain histamine showed signs behaviors that were similar to tics in humans.

Me: Strange.

We talked about all the sciencey stuff about Tourette's for a while. I brought up the ever so loved PANDAS and Ben seemed really intrigued by it. Then I brought up religion and learned that we had a lot more in common than I previously thought.

Me: So let me break a social norm and talk about religion. Did you go through any changes when you were diagnosed?

Ben: What do you mean?

Me: Like did officially "getting" Tourette's change your outlook on life and the universe?

Ben: When I was thirteen, fourteen I went through a really religious phase. I went to church a lot and was fairly conservative at the time.

Me: And then something changed?....

Ben: Yes. When I got kicked out of church I really felt like I was abandoned and after that I really fell away from the church.

Me: You got kicked out of church!? Why?

Ben: I said "Fuck me Jesus" pretty loud and several times.

Me: Ah. That would do it. But still it's a church for Christ's sake they should be more understanding of your condition.

Ben: I know. It was kind of a turning point in my faith. It was one day in Sunday school, in a tiny Baptist church. The kids were understanding (surprisingly) and they knew that "Ben just does and says stuff sometimes". However the priest there wasn't so understanding, And it was after one to many "Fuck me Jesuss" that he just got tired of me and told me to leave.

Me: That's terrible. I kind of know how you feel. One time I was on a train with friends. We were coming home from a day in the city when a couple of passengers asked the conductor to throw us off the train because I was making noises. Thankfully the other passengers had my back. But still, no one should be kicked out of anything, especially a church, for something that they cannot help.

Ben: I hear ya. The whole thing sparked a militant atheism phase in me.

Me: (Laughs) Ya I've been there. I went through that same phase myself right after being diagnosed.

Ben: Ya my boyfriend fixed that.

Me: Oh you are gay?

Ben: Yes. Well not really. Kinda. I like men and women.

Me: So you're bisexual?

Ben: Well I don't really like putting labels on it. If anything I'd say I'm pansexual.

Me: Well either way I'm glad you found someone. What's your boyfriends name?

Ben: Mitch.

Me: How'd you guys meet?

Ben: We met in a college class we both took about a year ago. I thought he was cute so I started talking to him. Asked if he wanted to hangout. We hung out a few times and then after one interesting night he asked me if we were dating now.

Me: (Laughs) Interesting night huh?

Ben: Ya (laughs) he's great it's like my tics aren't even an issue for him. To him I'm just another guy. I don't have a problem. I'm just me.

Me: That's awesome. You seem like a lucky guy. So what was it like realizing that you weren't straight? Anything you had to overcome?

Ben: You know it's a lot like having Tourette's. For a while you are in a sort of closet. You don't want anyone to know. You try to make excuses for your behavior whenever someone asks questions. You kind meet at a crossroads of sorts. You can either go one way and never accept it and the other way you finally come to terms with who you are and you become the person you were meant to be.

Me: That makes a lot of sense personally speaking. I used to work at an amphitheater as a security guard. Most of the time when my tics were bad people would ask me dumbass questions like "are you ok?" or "What's your problem?" I never really would ever just say "I have Tourette's you have a problem with that?" I don't know why I never "came out" like you said. Fear maybe? Could it be because I was afraid of how people would react after I said that? I don't know.

Ben: You probably were just afraid. I knew I was when I first came out. Both times (laughs)

Me: Have you ever had a time when someone got in your face about your tics? Like besides getting kicked out of church?

Ben: One time me and my friends were in Boston and I was getting dirty looks from one guy. My friends got in his face and defended me.

Me: Well that's great that you have such awesome friends.

Ben: Ya their pretty big queens so they were all flamboyant and snapping at the poor guy. It was quite the sight to see.

Me: I've found my friends to be a big source of backup for me. They have my back and I have theirs. It really is good that you have a support system that would stand up for you.

We talked about our friends for a while. Swapped some stories and told some tales about our many adventures in our respective cities. Friends are important to people like us. They're a support system. People you can rely on for help and backup.

Me: Tell me about your family.

Ben: They're there for me. We kind of adopted an easy going, funny approach to my tics.

Me: How so?

Ben: Like one day on my bus stop when I was in high school my brother texted me "Waffles" and kept saying it under his breath. Before I knew it I was yelling "WAFFLES" at the top of lungs uncontrollably.

Me: (Laughs) in all seriousness that sucks that it's that easy to change your tics.

Ben: Even more so when your brother tells you to do a nut punch.

Me: Yikes.

Ben: Ya but I still love him. He's in the air force now. Both he and my dad still say "Waffles" every now and then. Makes everyone laugh.

Me: You mentioned "nut punch". Has your tics ever caused you any pain?

(Ben arches his back and twitches his neck violently. I regret asking the question)

Ben: Well as you probably noticed I have some violent neck tics. I read something about getting Botox injections in the muscles that are effected.

Me: Really? I've never heard of that.

Ben: Ya it's supposed to be pretty effective. Once the muscles are injected they are paralyzed so any tics that are in that area never manifest again.

Me: That information could be very useful to anyone reading this conversation in a few years. Thanks.

Ben: Don't mention it. One time I also spent a week in the hospital
    because they were so bad.
Me: Damn. They got that bad huh?
Ben: It was awful. I missed a few days of school after that.
Me: Speaking of that; how was your school experience?
Ben: I mean it was okay I guess. Some people understood some
    didn't. I had to leave classes sometimes when they go really
    bad. One girl used to say shit like "faking it again to get out of
    class again?"
Me: What a twat.
Ben: (Laughs) certainly was. But my teachers understood. I never
    got in trouble or anything for them.
Me: Well considering some of the stuff you would say I'm glad you
    never got in trouble with anyone.
Ben: Oh you don't know the half of it. Sometimes I would just go
    up to people and say "Fuck off and die" or "I'll shave your pubes"
Me: … Did you ever shave anyone's pubes Ben?
Ben: (Laughs) NO! I'll admit it's a thing that not many people are
    used to hearing. I got some bizarre looks and reactions.
Me: I know my high school experience wasn't perfect. My tics
    weren't that bad at the time but occasionally I just couldn't hold
    them in.
Ben: I hear ya. My friends would sometimes make a game out of
    it. They made BINGO cards with different tics and whenever
    I would do one they would mark it down. So sometimes in the
    middle of class my friends would just yell "BINGO!"
Me: (Laughs) well I bet that made class interesting.
Ben: Certainly did.
Me: Did you or your family ever do anything weird to try to calm
    your tics? Like for example I went on a sugar free diet for a few
    months. It actually helped a bit but I weighed one hundred and
    twenty pounds at the end of it.
Ben: Wow. No we didn't ever do anything that extreme but speaking
    of food red dye seems to make it worse.
Me: Really now?

Ben: Yes which sucks because I love red skittles so much. I'm a fatass so I love my candy.

Me: Well at least you're burning calories as you sit still.

Ben: (Laughs) You know I never thought of it that way. Having Tourette's is a great way to lose weight isn't it.

Me: Sure is. That's why we are both in such great shape.

(I have the muscular structure of a baby bird)

Ben: Can I ask YOU a question?

Me: Of course. Shoot.

Ben: Do you find that smoking weed helps your tics at all?

Me: Of course! I smoke whenever I get the chance. Weed is a wonderful thing.

Ben: (Laughs) Ya I suppose it is.

Me: I mean it calms your body and weird shit happens and it's hilarious. Whenever I smoke with my friends I get all philosophical and talk about space.

Ben: Me and my friends just get high and usually watch *Fritz the Cat*.

Me and Ben talk about our weed based adventures for a while. Then we talk about space and *Cosmos* 'cause that's what good little stoners do.

Me: Well Ben that about raps it up. Thanks for talking to me today I really appreciate it.

Ben: No trouble at all thank YOU for talking to ME today.

Me: Anything you wanna add?

Ben: Yes actually. I remember a quote on Facebook I saw a while ago. It was like: "When you walk through the woods and see all the trees. You realize that some trees are different. Some are shorter than others. You don't feel bad for these trees. You accept them for who they are and keep walking." It went something like that I'm not sure who said it either.

Me: Huh. Interesting.

Ben: It just reminded me of when you said you used to be homophobic and that all changed once you were diagnosed. I once stayed in group housing for a bit. There were some people who were physically and mentally retarded. I was uncomfortable around them at first but then I learned to see past it. You see them as actual people.

Me: I know. Ever since I got sick I began to see things in a new light. People come in many different forms. What's important is that you see those forms and recognize them as people. I think that's the main problem with the world today. We don't see other people as actual people. We see them as the titles we give them. Republican, Democrat, White, Black, Gay, Straight. We should look past what makes us different. Our beliefs, our skin color, what we like, and just see fellow humans. Again, thanks a lot Ben.

Ben: You're welcome dude. Good luck on the book.

Me: Thanks.

I learned a lot from Ben during that interview. It's not something you forget, seeing someone like you. Someone who knows what you are going through. It certainly was a treat speaking to Ben and I encourage everyone reading this book to be more like him. See the world differently. Stop putting labels on other people and just see them for who they really are. Trust me, it makes the world a much better place when everyone in it is on the same team.

NOT-SO-GREAT-ESCAPE FROM A NOT-SO-GREAT-LIFE

If you only take one thing from this book let it be this: Having this illness isn't easy.

That's it.

That's all I want you to know.

Mainly because not enough people recognize that it's hard.

Tourette's is comedy fodder.

It's used as a funny comic relief in the media.

But it really shouldn't be.

Because it's really fucking hard to deal with.

I'm not being overly sensitive about it.

South Park did an excellent job portraying it in that one episode. I can admit that.

In all honesty I thought the episode was pretty funny.

Anyway if you have this disease and your anything like me then you probably aren't excelling in the social areas.

Or maybe you're nothing like me and don't let a silly sickness get you down and you rock and roll all night and/or party every day.

Maybe you don't see the bad in people and you stand up for yourself and you love life.

Maybe you're just this perfect human being.

Or maybe you're not.

And you're just like me.

I've always been a weird kid.

I think I mentioned that in the beginning of this book.

Was I a social kid in my pre-tourette's life?

Not really.

In preschool I hung onto my mother's leg as she tried to walk me through the door.

I waited a year to join preschool.

I don't know exactly why.

Maybe holding onto my mother's leg as she tried to walk was a big indicator that I wasn't ready for school yet.

So I've always been the oldest in any class despite being small too.

It's a strange paradox. Being old and small.

Kind of like the old man from *UP* (his name was Carl)

Anyway I can remember starting preschool pretty well.

I remember playing with the dinosaur toys in the corner.

I wasn't really into playing with other kids.

I mean if they were playing the same thing I was then ya sure I'll play with you.

But you start doing something I don't like?

Then were not playing anymore.

My mom would say "I walk to the beat of my own drum"

I would say I just don't like people that much.

What I did like was getting lost in my own imagination.

I could make anything fun and exciting.

Long car rides, running errands with my parents.

What I would do was simply pretend I was doing something else.

Getting a new piece of equipment for the pool?

I was really getting a high tech artifact that would help Earth win against an Alien force.

Going on a trip to the museum?

I was meeting at the compound of human refugees after the apocalypse.

I could make anything fun.

Even school.

Especially school.

In school I was in a futuristic military training camp.

Simple math turned into high end physics class.

Gym class turned into life or death exercises.

Science was alien anatomy.

Art was just Art.

I didn't make anything cool out of art class.

I called this realm of imagination "adventures".

Solely out of boredom I would pretend to be somewhere else.

I did this a lot when I was alone.

And I would be alone a lot.

Either I had no one to hang out with or I just didn't feel like hanging out with the few people who actually did.

Sometimes I get in this mood where I just don't want to see anybody all day.

I sit and play video games or watch television all day.

I don't know why I got in those moods.

I could say that I was embarrassed about my tics and didn't want to go out and socialize, but that wouldn't make sense since I would act like that in my pre-tic days.

My parents (and myself) believe I fit somewhere on the autism-spectrum.

Because I don't have enough on my plate.

❦

I get the sense that I am not that much of a well-liked person.

Call me paranoid, but I feel like I have enough experience in this field to tell when I'm not wanted.

Maybe it's just my personality.

I am kind of an immature douche bag.

Sometimes I say the wrong things at the wrong time.

And by sometimes I mean at least once every social event I'm actually invited to.

I like to think my awkwardness started at a very young age.

I mentioned before how I took a year off preschool because I wanted to stay home and watch *Blue's Clues*.

My mother says I wasn't "ready" for school yet.

I think not being ready for school is a big indicator of being a weirdo.

I mean I do have some charisma.

It just shows up when it wants to.

I had my first girlfriend at four years old.

Does that really count though?

I mean we did kiss.

Yes, I had my first kiss at four years old.

Should I really count that as a "girlfriend"?

We would pretend we were married.

We would play "Flintstones", where we would play house with our socks off.

For some reasons being barefoot and staying in a playhouse translated to being the Flintstones.

I went to two different preschools.

My first preschool was in called "Butterfly Garden".

It was a nice little place.

Then we moved to a town called Orland Park, where I went to a place called "Sandbox".

I remember being afraid of a kid with a skin tag on his chin.

Anyway I also remember this music teacher.

She would make us build our own snacks and then we would eat them.

Sounds pretty nice?

One time we were making marshmallow spiders for a Halloween treat and she made us use black licorice for the legs. I simply said I don't like black licorice cause who does?

It tastes like poison and especially for a little kid.

She says: "Tyler ... you make me sad when you say that."

What the hell lady?

Why would you guilt trip a little kid because he doesn't like your nasty ass snack?

It's black licorice for Christ's sake.

No little kid likes black licorice.

Hell I'm pretty sure not many adults like black licorice either.

Anyway that was the highlight of my preschool career.

Next (obviously) came Kindergarten.

This is where I some of my first real friends. Luke and Adam.

I also became really attached to an alligator puppet in my class.

I don't know why.

Just thought it looked cool.

It was a green puppet with a big yellow letter A on its tummy.

And it looked like an alligator.

Had little velvet teeth and everything.

It was just a cool puppet.

I remember my first unreciprocated crush too. Which was also in Kindergarten.

Amy was her name.

I would tell you her last name but I don't want to get sued.

I had a huge crush on her and represented it by harassing her and just being a general nuisance.

Now one could argue that since I was six years old, this shouldn't be a reflection of my personality and I should stop beating myself up for it.

But then we would have no story to tell.

I can't help but beat myself up (both mentally and physically) because it shows what kind of person I would become to be.

The kind of person who seems something good and subconsciously decides to sabotage it.

I don't mean to.

I just do what I do.

"My brain hates me" is the leading theory I have.

Anyway Amy was just the first one in a long line of obsession and rejection.

In first grade it was Isabelle.

Why didn't that one turn out well?

Well that's because my "best friend" at the time told her I pissed my pants on the bus.

The fucked up thing?

I actually did....

Because I thought it was funny.

I didn't just lose control of my bladder.

I just pissed my pants for no reason.

And yes for some reason I was still his friend after he told about my pee escapades.

Why?

Because I didn't (still don't) have much self-esteem and I took all the friends I could possibly get and keep.

In second grade my love interest was Courtney.

We used to do this weird thing as kids where the boys would chase the girls throughout the playground.

Looking back that was kind of creepy but then again we were eight years old and maybe I'm just being too hard on myself.

I would chase Courtney around the park.

But the thing is: "What would I do if I actually caught her?"

I have no clue.

I didn't plan for that.

I just chased her.

And she ran.

Never did she ever just stop and wonder what would happen if I caught up to her.

Well neither did I.

And the thing is when recess was over we just stopped chasing each other and walk back together back to class.

Like nothing weird happened at all during recess.

I made me think that deep down those girls wanted to be chased.

Because why not?

It was just another form of human interaction.

A stupid form, but human interaction its purest form.

And no I'm not saying that girls love this because they love attention.

I'm saying that people, especially kids, love any form of attention that isn't completely negative.

I think that's why I, as an incredibly awkward person, say stupid things.

Because I get noticed for it.

I can't count how many times I've been totally ignored at parties or other social gatherings and have acted out just to be noticed.

Is that a normal thing to do?

Like am I the only person who sometimes acts like an idiot because he or she is not getting any attention.

If it makes you feel better to know I don't really do that anymore.

Now I just sit there in silence when I'm being ignored.

Usually someone attempts to talk to me and then I break my silence.

But not often.

In third grade I called my teacher "Mom".

That's not really important to anything I just thought it was funny.

Embarrassing but funny.

Fourth grade was when things really started to change for me.

And by that I mean I realized that I was the dweeb.

I had a crush on a girl named Lexi back then.

The girl of the year that I would never get.

Everyone knew too which made it more embarrassing.

This was also the grade where I started getting bullied.

I never had a problem with other kids before this so it came as quite a shock.

That people will not like you for whatever reason they find acceptable.

I was chunky.

That was my sin.

I also liked to read.

Who makes fun of a kid for reading?

You basically admit that you're making fun of me because I'm smarter than you.

But I think being chunky had more to do with it.

I was also pretty short too.

Chunky and short are not the greatest of combinations.

I was like one of those little rolly polly beetles.

Shy, chubby and small.

It wasn't until junior high that I realized how unpopular I was.

I was picked on a lot in sixth grade.

One time I got shoved to the ground because I wasn't good at football.

I dreaded gym class.

I wasn't good at anything because I was so out of shape.

I was picked last all the time.

It's something I got used to but it still hurt when it happened.

The only person who got picked after me was the kid who was born premature.

Sixth grade is an interesting time for a child's life.

Puberty is starting so hormones are everywhere.

Testosterone is through the roof so all the boys are violent little sociopaths.

And all the girls are moody bitches.

I was kind of a late bloomer so I wasn't aggressive like the other boys.

I never wanted to fight anyone or act up in class to impress the girls.

And people noticed that.

For some reason, if you're shy and awkward, everyone assumes you're gay.

I'm not sure how many times I was called "faggot" in junior high, but it sure felt like a lot.

It's a stigma that I've carried throughout my life and well into high-school.

For some reason most people just assume that I like penises.

There's nothing wrong with liking penises, it's just that it's not for me.

I love my own but that about sums it up for penises that I enjoy.

Anyway ya I wasn't well liked in sixth grade.

This created a sort of paradox.

I wasn't liked so I tried to be funny, which made more people hate me, which made me try to be funnier.

I think it stemmed from the one time I got a laugh.

The kid's name was Kyle and he was one of the popular kids in school.

He laughed at a joke I made and that destined me to try again with everyone else.

That started my obsession with comedy.

An obsession with trying to make people laugh.

There was an article I read about comedy by David Wong (author of *John Dies at the End*, one of the greatest comedy/horror novels of all time).

In the article he explains why funny people are so miserable.

We are awkward individuals who, at one point, make someone laugh, and we latch onto that.

Am I funny?

Do I have the right to include myself in that group of "Funny people"?

I don't know, it seems like I make some people laugh.

Hopefully I made you chuckle once or twice during this book, otherwise it may seem very depressing for both of us.

Anyway I made Kyle laugh at thus started my fixation on trying to be funny.

Of course I wasn't funny.

It was just an attempt to make kids like me.

The thing is I was "funny" at the expense of others.

I talked a lot of shit about people.

I would talk shit about person A to person B, then talk shit about person B to person A.

You get what I'm saying?

I was so desperate for attention that I burned most of the very few social bridges I had built.

Do no talk shit about people.

I can't stress that enough.

No good comes out of it.

If you don't like someone, be honest about it.

Don't act like their your friend and then turn around and gossip about them behind their backs.

I did that and it got me nowhere.

I lost a lot of friends that way.

And I can never take back what I said about those people.

That whole phrase "Sticks and stone may break my bones, but words can never hurt me"?

Bullshit.

Words have impact.

Words have power.

Words can ruin somebody's day.

Words can ruin somebody's life.

That's why I had about three friends in junior high.

And the fucked up thing was?

We talked shit about each other all the time.

One time my friend Jeremy made me sit outside our friend Jon's house and listen to him talk shit about us.

That's the shit I was dealing with as I was going through puberty.

As if I didn't have enough on my plate.

I can remember asking her for her AIM address.

You see kids, back in the day before texting there was this thing called AIM which stood for "AOL instant messaging". AOL stood for "America Online." You would type your words in a little box and then send it to the recipient. And they would type back. It was very primitive and stupid yet everybody did it. Probably because back in the day, everyone was primitive and stupid.

I was incredibly nervous.

I asked her for her AIM she said "I'd need to write it down"

Luckily I was prepared like a good little social awkward nerd.

I brought a post-it note and a pencil with me on the bus ride home.

Surprisingly she didn't laugh in my face.

Though her friend did.

And I was chatting with her that night.

We talked about a lot of stuff and from what I remember, I didn't say anything too stupid.

This was before my tics were really noticeable so I had more self-confidence than I should have for a chubby nerd.

It doesn't really matter what I said.

It was just another failed conquest.

A failed attempt at a relationship.

Who would want to date me?

I was a nobody.

Either way, by seventh grade I was more in shape.

I had picked up martial arts.

I really did enjoy doing martial arts (it was Tae Kwon Doe for your information)

It was a release from my daily life.

I could act out on my stress and insecurities.

Beat the shit out of a punching bag or padded mat.

I actually got my black belt.

It wasn't that big of an achievement.

One hundred pushups.

One hundred sit ups.

A mile run.

And a few moves from your previous belts.

And you had to break a few boards.

Nothing that hard, but for me back then? It might as well be a decathlon.

But I still accomplished it.

Even though it was fat kid repellant I still did it.

And I felt good about it.

Because while it may be easy to do now, it certainly wasn't easy back then.

In fact, I kinda wish I still did martial arts.

It would probably be a nice therapy for tics.

Stress reliever?

Check.

Teaches you discipline and concentration?

Check.

Wearing comfy clothes?

Double check. (Have you ever felt one of those uniforms?)

I would highly recommend martial arts for anyone with tics.

In fact I recommend it for anyone really.

It helped me deal with a lot of shit in my past.

But enough about that.

Just take that with a grain of salt and try it out one day.

Even if you're old it's not that embarrassing going to karate class.

Either way, by seventh grade I was more in shape.

The only problem was, I was still an awkward asshole.

But now I was a skinny asshole.

This trend would continue to this very day.

I coasted through eighth grade, gaining some friends surprisingly along the way.

I left my junior high with open arms, ready to take on the future that was high school.

I was going to reinvent myself.

I was going to become a different person.

And of course, then life comes along and slaps you in the face.

I started off my freshman year thinking I had reinvented myself.

Then I had to give a speech about an accomplishment we had done.

I decided to talk about losing weight.

That didn't go so well.

I stuttered and stammered and sounded like a dork.

Not the best way to start off the year.

Especially the year I was supposed to reinvent myself.

Really all I did my freshman year was get a girlfriend (shocked I know) and then be miserable with her.

Sam was an interesting girl.

Not quite right in the head.

That, or just desperate for attention.

Really we were a perfect match for each other.

We met on Halloween at a bonfire a few mutual friends were having.

We flirted and talked and had a pretty good time.

We talked on AIM (This was still a thing surprisingly)

I asked her to a school dance one day.

We actually enjoyed ourselves.

I kissed her for the first time that night.

Anyway, that relationship was doomed to fail.

We were both crazy.

I'm pretty sure she still hates me.

Would I say I was in an abusive relationship?

Well I did get hit a lot.

And constantly accused of cheating (even though I would never do such a thing)

We fought all the time.

I don't really know if I consider that abusive, but I would consider it a bad relationship.

If you're anything like me, then you're so single that you don't know how to act when in a relationship.

You have to meet parents and their friends that aren't your friends.

You have to act accordingly and not be a douchebag even though you know they be talking shit about you.

Seriously fuck you Nathan, you fat little shit. You don't even know me and you're just jealous that she didn't like you back.

Okay that may just be a problem that I specifically had.

My point is, if you're new to the dating scene, don't sweat it.

Just don't act superior or tell your significant other what to do all the time or hit them or be mean to them.

And don't cheat.

Ever.

You're an asshole if you cheat and I don't feel sorry for you if you get dumped because you had that coming.

Girlfriends/boyfriends are just normal friends that occasionally rub body parts.

So treat them like friends and don't hurt them.

Physically or emotionally.

I can't really give any more advice on dating since I've been single for years.

And I've dated like three girls total.

So I'm just going to continue talking about my journey through high school.

My sophomore year was my best.

I was on the track team and I was working out more.

I was in fantastic shape.

Of course what I'm really saying here is that I peaked in sophomore year of high school.

I had dozens of friends and was never bored or alone.

I was feeling on top of the world.

Then came Junior year.

That's when my tics started to manifest into hardcore physical tics.

It was bad enough I started losing friends.

I'm still not sure if that was because of my tics or because insert generic high school drama bullshit here.

It certainly didn't help my self-esteem no matter what it was for sure.

The thing is when one day you're normal (or at least somewhat normal) and the next you have really bad tics, people take notice.

I don't know if more people pitied me or were annoyed by me.

Either way it still hurt.

I want to take a small step to the side and talk about a kid named Nick.

I bullied Nick.

A lot.

The thing is he kind of had it coming.

He was so desperate for friends that he would do anything, like talk behind people's backs and try to put people down in front of others.

Sound familiar?

He also bought weed and sold it back to eighth graders at the price he bought it for.

Ya he wasted money just so kids would buy weed from him.

Even I never did anything that desperate.

Regardless, I made fun of this kid because he was like me.

And I hated me.

I took my own personal hatred for myself out on this kid because he reminded me so much of myself.

I would make fun of his scoliosis and the way he spat when he said his S's.

I think the reason I hated him so much was because the way he talked about other kids.

He made fun of my friend John's stutter and we reacted by both punching him in the balls.

The thing is he just wouldn't get the hint that there was a reason we tormented him.

Much like how I never got the hint in junior high that I was an unfunny douche.

One time in biology class, my friends and I saw a peculiar square on the floor.

Turns out it was a Maxi pad.

We opened it and I drew a little red splotch on it with a marker.

I should point out that Nick wore a back brace. And therefor couldn't feel it if you touched his back.

I volunteered to do what you are already piecing together.

I walked up behind Nick and slapped him on the back.

"Hey man, what are you doing this weekend?" I exclaimed.

He started to answer, but I wasn't listening.

I didn't really care.

Come to think of it, I'm not sure why he didn't suspect anything was going on.

Why would I care what he did this weekend?

Just a few weeks prior I put his binder in the sink and had another kid turn it on.

I walked away giggling like a maniac.

My friends stood at the classroom door out in the hallway, watching this unfold.

I didn't know this at the time but Nick's next class was at the opposite end of the school.

Our school housed four thousand kids.

Nick walked the entire length of the school with a maxi pad attached to his back.

And it was all me.

I tortured that kid throughout high school even with my tics.

I think it got worse when my tics started because I was angry and needed to vent.

That or I really am just an asshole.

Anyway let's talk about drugs now.

Junior year is when I discovered the magic of alcohol and weed and how to drown your sorrows in them.

One of my friends started smoking weed in junior year of high school.

Which was strange because before that he was so against the very concept of smoking weed.

Then again so was I at the time.

The first time I tried it was the winter of Junior year, only a few months after being diagnosed.

Back then I really wanted to go to this nightclub that was for kids.

It was called Zero Gravity, and it was made for people sixteen years old and up.

Why did I want to go to this pedophile haven?

Because I was so desperate for human connection I wanted to do 'what everyone else was doing'.

And yes in my generic midwestern town this nightclub was what a lot of people did.

Anyway we are getting ready to go to this club.

We are driving around my friend's neighborhood when he stresses the fact that he really doesn't want to go to this club.

I call him a pussy and insist that he comes along.

He makes a deal with me: Smoke weed with him and he'll go with.

I really want him to come along.

So I gave in.

I tried pot for the first time in my life.

And you know what?

I had a blast.

We smoked out of a pen.

Crudely made and stupid, it was just a one-hitter that shot clumps of weed in the back of your throat whenever you tried to smoke out of it.

We finished all the weed we had and drove around the block to air out my friend's car.

We finally arrived at our destination, our friend's house, where we were to meet up with everyone else who was going to the club with us.

When we stood on her porch and rang her doorbell I started laughing, and couldn't stop.

My cheeks turned bright red as I wheezed and tried to breath.

I was really laughing my ass off over something that was a normal event. (If you call junior nightclubs normal events)

She opens the door to see me laughing hysterically.

"You guys smoked didn't you?"

Back then it was sort of taboo to smoke, especially around adults.

Knowing her parents were home and could confront us at any minute (why the hell would they?) was a risk that we were willing to take, but made all the sober ones uneasy.

It's at this point that my friend I just made a deal with decides to head home, backing out of our deal to go to this club and get that sweet attention from strangers we truly didn't care about.

He really did not want to go it seems.

We get in our cars (I can't drive, I am currently tripping balls) and head off to the town Naperville, where the shady nightclub Zero Gravity awaits.

I am starring at the headlights, looking at the spectacular light show unfolding before me.

It's about an hour drive.

I don't even notice how long it takes.

We arrive at the club and mind you that it's about thirty degrees outside.

We pull up in our parking space and I see two young girls in tank tops and shorts that are basically just underwear walk in the place.

We enter the club and it's surprisingly packed.

The rest of the night, from my memory anyway, goes by in a blur.

I danced like an idiot and I looked like one too.

There was elevated center piece in the middle of the dance floor.

So of course I go up on it and dance with some Filipino chick.

I don't remember much else.

I remember dancing with a few different chicks.

I remember getting rejected by a few different chicks.

I remember that water cost like three fucking dollars in that place.

I remember seeing a lot of older guys in that place which was sobering and creepy as hell.

And I remember being told by some guy that if I needed anybody killed, he's the guy to call.

So that pretty much guaranteed that I would never go there again.

That and being told by my friends that they were never going again.

So I never went to another club again.

And you know what?

I'm glad.

Am I just bitter because I had a lousy time and a poorly run, creepy club?

Probably.

Anyway that was the first I tried pot.

Let's talk about the first time I drank.

It was the summer time and I spent more time with my friend Max than with my other friends.

Max was a lazy drunk, but I loved that kid.

I felt like he was one of the few kids who understood what I was dealing with when my tics became really bad.

Max introduced me to booze.

And I fell into a deep and terrible, but lovely, relationship with it.

We first just started drinking in Max's basement.

Just little things, nothing too crazy.

Then we would drink more.

And more.

And more.

And then I stopped remembering.

One time I drank too much and something actually bad happened.

A fourth of July party.

My sister bought us the booze and we shelled out quite a lot of money for it.

But we didn't care.

We just wanted to get fucked up.

I arrived at her house and guess who's there?

None other than my ex from Freshman year.

Mind you we have been broken up for two years.

And I bet some of you sharper ones reading this can already guess where this is going.

Anyway she just got out of another long relationship with another guy.

He dumped her ass and she was rightfully upset.

So she decided to drink herself stupid.

And I just got diagnosed with Tourette's, so I was depressed.

So I decided to drink myself stupid.

It was my idea to build a fort in the basement.

We got together tables and blankets and couch cushions and built a pretty damn good fort if I don't say so myself.

And she won't leave me alone.

She's clinging onto me and won't let go..

I think it was because of Rory.

Freshly dumped, she just wasn't over him and the alcohol in her was skewing her judgment.

I am shitfaced. So I retire to the fort to be alone for a while.

She decides to follow me.

I'm not proud of what happened. But it did lead to one good thing. No matter how ashamed about what I did in there, no matter how you judge me, that shameful night did lead to one good thing.

It lead to the birth of my son Jeffery, and I'll never forget that night.

Totally kidding.

We passed out because we were children and couldn't handle alcohol.

I also puked a lot.

I puke almost every time I drink because I NEED to go hard.

Like I have something to prove other than I am stupid.

The thing is I don't learn.

I have one drink and can't stop.

Senior year was a tough time for me.

It was my last year of high school.

I would be going to college soon.

And I was not mentally prepared to go to college yet.

It was like preschool all over again.

Except this time mommy's not gonna hold my hand on the way out.

I didn't really care about anything during senior year.

My grades dropped significantly.

I only went to parties to drown myself in vodka.

And I started to lose friends again.

Plus this is when the IVIG I mentioned earlier started to wear off, so imagine thinking that one day all your troubles are going to go away and then that just never happens.

I was pretty devastated.

It didn't help either that I got rejected to prom.

The girl I was going to go with turned around at the last minute and told me to go with her friend instead.

I did, but I was still pissed.

At least karma had my back on that one since her date left her at the dance.

That was kind of cool.

But then again I got food poisoning from eating prom food so maybe karma didn't have my side.

Seriously if you haven't gone to prom yet and they have food prepared for you, don't eat it.

Learn from my mistake.

Anyway that's how my senior year of high school ended.

Me depressed and becoming a lazy drunk.

Oh ya I also smoke a ton of weed to hide my depression.

In case you forgot, that one time I did it so my friend would come to the club with me was far from the last time.

I smoked every time I had to chance.

Nearly every weekend.

One time we made edibles in my kitchen when my parents weren't home.

They were called firecrackers.

They were consisted of graham crackers, peanut butter, and weed.

We brought them to a Relay for Life event at my school once.

I made Jell-O-shots.

Well, it was more of a tub of alcoholic Jell-O than individual shots but you get the idea.

If you don't know what Relay for Life is, it's an organization that raises money for cancer research.

It's a big thing for my school and a pretty sacred event for some people who lost family members to cancer.

So we responded to this solemn event by getting fucked up or fucked.

Seriously, a lot of people get it on at these events.

I hooked up with a girl who was in a relationship and I knew this but didn't care.

I was mentally checked out.

I also spent the rest of the night sleeping on the cold, hard ground cause our tent wouldn't fit on the grass because we got there so late.

Karma I guess?

Another time I had fun with firecrackers was this time I went out in the woods with some friends and starred at a creek for half an hour.

Another time I ate my last quarter on the firecracker and went to go get pizza.

I saw another kid there.

His name was Andrew, and I used to bully him too.

I started getting really hot.

I stared sweating and my head hurt.

My vision got blurry.

I don't know why I freaked out at the sight of this kid.

Maybe because I was guilty that I used to give him such a hard time?

I don't know, weed makes you do some weird shit.

Oh ya, then I puked.

The fucked up thing is I haven't learned my lesson.

I still drink.

I still smoke.

I try to contain myself and do it in moderation.

I think I'm getting better at it too.

It's just that it makes my tics go away.

Or at least makes me forgot about them for awhile.

I'm not self-conscious when I am drunk or high.

But the thing is I should be because I act like an ass when I'm either one of those.

Don't be like me.

Don't drown your sorrows in a something, whatever it may be.

It's not healthy to depend on a substance.

Drink a little with your friends.

It's normal.

Light up one day with some friends, just to mellow out.

It's normal too.

Just don't over indulge in it like I did.

If you have Tourette's or literally any other problem, booze is not the answer to your problems.

Drink to have fun not to forget.

It's a slippery slope.

Cause all you're gonna do is create more awful memories that you're gonna want to forget.

It's a downward spiral.

One that I can insist is something you should never do.

Same goes for marijuana.

Just chill out, don't go crazy.

Weed actually seems to help tics so I recommend it.

Just, and I can't stress it enough, do not rely on it.

Life is good.

Generally.

We don't need a substance in order to get by.

We can get through the hard times on our own.

Without a crutch.

So if you have a problem, be it being a little twitchy or depressed, don't turn to the bottle.

It just leads to more problems.

Not to mention you're strong enough to get by without it.

I have faith in you, complete stranger.

You can be better than me.

We are only human.

We make mistakes.

But there is no sense in doing something that will just lead to more mistakes.

That's just silly.

KAYLEY'S STORY

Kayley was born in 1995.

She lives in Lucama, North Carolina.

Kayley helped write that *Cracked.com* article I'm so found about.

I requested that we talk via Skype for this interview and she (obviously) said yes.

I was really excited to talk to a girl with Tourette's since it's pretty uncommon.

Boys are four times as likely to haves symptoms than girls.

Anyway without further ado here is Kayley's story.

Me: When did you first have your tics?

Kayley: Since I was about seven years old.

Me: What were your first tics? Like what did you do?

Kayley: My first tic that I can remember was biting the inside of my cheeks. And rubbing my ankles together.

Me: I read in our *Cracked.com* article that you needed a wheelchair. When did they get so severe?

Kayley: When I was fourteen it went from mild to moderate to extremely severe. I was in band class one morning and my arms started jerking and over the next week more and more tics came. Like the swearing, full body jerking, hitting myself, etc. It just got worse and worse for no reason anybody could see. I got sent home from school because I couldn't hold a pencil, and didn't go back for a year because it stayed that bad. Actually, kept getting worse and worse. And the drugs? … gosh.

Me: That's terrible. When my first tics started to come into play I felt that certain things made them worse. Sugar, alcohol, and especially stress. Do you think it was any of those that set you off?

Kayley: Yes (laughs) My personal theory after dozens of experts were like "meh we have no idea" sort of thing, is that my OCD, which became debilitating, like major depression kind of bad, and went untreated for more than a year. The sort of OCD I have is like guilty thoughts and sad stuff, so I didn't tell anybody for a long time. I think the extreme stress of that just sort of made things go haywire. I mean there's reports of the same sort of deal going on in others who were milder and then had exacerbations also. Anyway, things that make them worse? Well just about everything (Laughs) exercise, excitement, laughing, sleep deprivation, overstimulation, and stress of any sort. Yeah pretty much anything good will set them off. Or did at least.

Me: Wow. OCD definitely has a part of it. Sometimes I feel like I can't tell what's a tic and what is OCD.

Kayley: Oh man, I drive myself crazy trying to like, pick apart tics and the suggestibility aspect of it. Certain doctors have accused me of faking or like it being all mental before and that just fed the OCD so I will like obsess over whether any of it is like suggestible and stuff. I've been doing much better since I had DBS, it's kind of weird really.

Me: Oh you had DBS? Tell me about that.

Kayley: So… its a very long story. As everything with me is (Laughs). But here's the short version.

Me: I want the long version (Laughs).

(WARNING: MANY SCIENCE WORDS ARE COMING UP)

Kayley: I was fourteen within a month of my exacerbation, we went to John Hopkins to see Harvey Singer, that was supposed to be a Tourette's expert.(Laughs) Not as expert as he'd like you to think. And after clonidine/guanfacine did nothing. Risperdal made me sleep twenty-four seven at the minimum dose, and three days of minimum dose Fluphenazine landed me in the ER with acute dystonia (muscle contractions) with opisthotonus (a state of severe hyperextension and spasticity in which an individual's head, neck and spinal column enter into a complete "bridging" or "arching" position.) (Thanks Wikipedia!) And Haldol caused orofacial dyskinesia (involuntary repetitive movements of the mouth and face), he (Dr. Singer) well, told my local doctor "There's always DBS" who told my mom who eventually told me because I was in such a bad place that it was like seriously I want to die. So we watched a video of a girl from Australia who had it done.

Me: And that had you sold on it?

Kayley: I was amazed. First she looked almost exactly like me with the tics. And I'd never seen anybody like me. It looked like it caused a remission for her. Although later I'd find out later that she isn't doing very well at all. Wouldn't find that out until much, much later. Like six months ago today later. And it's worth mentioning now, I'm 19 so it's been quite a while. That was my first knowledge of it, and it was a pretty exciting idea given I spent most of the day convulsing, swearing, hitting, biting and kicking myself in between weird episodes of paralysis, which would turn out to be psychogenic, which means basically my brain was saying "Hey you, stop beating me up"

Me: That's incredible. I've never heard of that before.

Kayley: Yeah so I became obsessed with the idea of it. It's supposedly rare, and as James F. Leckman (a rock-star in the Tourette world from Yale. He even has his own Wikipedia page) once said I have a "unique" case. Which is not something you want to hear from an expert (Laughs). However it seems more common than one would think. In fact several people I know online have had it. One local doctor and my therapist believe its part of Tourette's syndrome.

Me: I mean I've had tics where my entire movement stops but I wouldn't call it being paralyzed.

Kayley: I personally think that past a certain point your brain will do whatever it can to save itself even if it means freaking you the heck out because you collapse getting back into the car from the parking lot in Walmart or on the dining room floor or whatever. Basically it induced paralysis because that was the only way I'd stop hurting myself. The human brain is so incredibly complex and so smart. But as to what you were saying you experienced? Brief episodes of inability to move? Like freezing? That's known as blocking, or blocking of movement. It's considered a tic. It's on the YGTSS for one.

Me: What is the YGTSS?

Kayley: Yale Global Tic Severity Scale.

Me: I had no idea there was a scale for that.

Kayley: You fill out this long questionnaire and it gives doctors a numerical value for severity. One to one hundred. And before my DBS my score was ninety five.

Me: Holy Shit.

Kayley: Yeah. I had a friend whose score was ninety nine.

Me: What is your score now?

Kayley: I'm not sure. I think I'm considered "Marked" now rather than shit a brick severe. Although now my symptoms are more episodic in nature which makes it a little hard to follow the scale.

Me: Has the DBS made a decent difference?

Kayley: Oh definitely! Or at least I want to believe that. Y'Know, having undergone brain surgery and stuff the whole cognitive dissonance thing, wanting to believe it's helped might be responsible for some of the improvement. But anyway my mom thinks I'm seventy percent better.

Me: God once you start to going into the brain shit gets so weird.

Kayley: Everything's weird. Tourette's wise especially.

Me: How does your family react to it?

Kayley: My family's awesome. Without them I probably would've offed myself by now. I went through some extremely rough patches and so did they. My med reactions were hell. Just horrific. Like stuff you wouldn't think was possible. That and just the living like you're going through rounds with yourself… and the wall… and the house… all the time does a number on everybody.

Me: What were your reactions again? Less sciency words this time so we don't scare off any slow readers.

Kayley: Would you like a spreadsheet? I've been on so many drugs.

- Clonidine/Guanfacien didn't do much of anything by the time I was fourteen and my tics got so bad. I've been on it for several years to manage milder tics and insomnia at that point.
- Risperdal just made me sleep all day. Take a dose at lunch and I'd sleep till five in the afternoon.
- Fluphenazine/Pimozide was horrific. I woke up one morning into three days taking it at minimum dose, just didn't feel right. Then while I was eating breakfast my head turned to the side so I went to lie down to try to make my head go right and then the rest of my body started kinking up too. My back arched backwards and stayed stuck, my eyes pulled back and up into my head so I could barley see, my jaw spasmed and so did my tongue and I could barley talk so I started drooling and vomiting, and my neck and body hurt because everything was so tight.

After calling my doctor and trying a Benadryl, my mom called my dad who drove me to the ER where they put in an IV and gave me benztropine and Benadryl.

Me: …. I'm taking pimozide now. Damn.

Kayley: The benztropine and Benadryl stopped all of the spasms in twenty mintues. It's called "acute dystonic reaction". Dystonic referring to abnormal muscle tone. Dye meaning bad and ton referring to the tone of the muscles. Mine was extremely severe.

Most people who get them have their head pull to the side for a bit. Mine was generalized meaning full body, with this wicked thing they call opsithotonus which is full body arching and ocyloguyric crisis which means your eyes pull off to one side or up. And the vomiting, they said that was stomach muscle spasms. That was our first WTF moment with drugs really.

Me: I used to vomit a lot too. I would hit myself in the stomach so hard I would just spew liquid hamburger everywhere.

Kayley: (Laughs) I thought I was dying needless to say. It really scared me.

Me: Sounds scary.

Kayley: One time I screamed so much eventually everything just came back up with the next scream (Laughs). And I have this puking tic. Well tic, or some other thing. You know how it is trying to delineate which is which with Tourette's.

Me: Ya I mentioned my OCD before, sometimes it feels like my face is uneven and I have to punch it to "fix" it.

Kayley: Sometimes I'd kick myself in one shin and then have to kick the other because it was like, not right. Because both sides have to hurt.

Me: ya right? I could never understand that.

Kayley: Tourette's and OCD are evil, plain and simple (Laughs).

Me: It's like a Yin and Yang made of shit.

Kayley: It's like seriously hurting myself once isn't enough?

Me: When this all stared, did your outlook on life change? Like for I went through various philosophical phases trying to justify what was happening.

Kayley: I became pretty depressed. Like when it got really bad. Passive suicidal kind of depressed. Course, a lot of what happened to me it's hard to say if it was drugs or just how I was coping. I would go on and off of them so many times. Although the worst was Topamax.

Me: Ya I've been there. Topamax sucks. Although I must admit I hate talking about my own tics to you because mine were never so bad. Like I have no room to complain.

Kayley: Well I really don't compare to some of my friends. Two of them could have basically died from their tics. What have yours been like?

Me: They've changed so much. The big one was hitting myself. I caused cauliflower ear in my left ear. It only happens to professional fighters (Laughs).

Kayley: Yikes.

Me: And I can't see out of my left eye. It's always really blurry.

Kayley: That sucks. One tic that drives me crazy affects my vision because I will like squeeze my eyes shut that or my eyes will pull back in my head. Of course this love to happen when I'm driving.

Me: Of course (Laughs) I hate when I tic while driving which is pretty self-explanatory. I just hate the thought of causing an accident and it being my fault.

Kayley: A little obsessive thought here or there like oh what if I did this? And then you have the urge and then you're fighting it as much as possible. And the thing is, I rarely suppress my tics while driving. It's like coordinating an insane dance.

Me: I get that urge you're talking about. Expect mine is like "What if I hurt this person?"

Kayley: Last night I was in line at this convenience store and I like flashed back to a couple months ago before surgery, how the whole time in line I'd been fighting the urge to hit this kid who was like standing right beside me.

Me: It plays like a little movie in your head. The scenario of just smacking someone in the face just to see what would happen.

Kayley: Yeah. And then it's like "urge ... go away". For me urges are like, feelings in part of my body. Say thinking of hitting I get urges in my forearm. And they're also cognitive like a concept in my head of like what I'm about to do, is about to happen.

Me: I like to think of it as a mental tic. Your brain misfiring and random thoughts come up. I don't know how scientific that actually is but....

Kayley: More or less (Laughs) The physiology of urges would be extremely interesting.

Me: Ya tell me about it.

Kayley: NIH had a study in the works to determine if the urges were present in the peripheral nervous system, the central, or both.

Me: Really? Tell me about that.

Kayley: Like they'd numb a subjects hand or wherever they're urgey with lidocaine and see if they'd still feel it. And they'd measure with EMG the local impulses in the body part and were going to do TMS later to see if they could induce urges. It's been awhile since I read about the study I'm sure I could find it online again.

Me: I'm sure I'll find it later.

(I searched later to only find the description on clinicaltrials.gov which means it's most likely still in progress. But hey by the time you're reading this it may be out there.)

Me: Now when I asked earlier if your outlook on life changed and you said you became really depressed, how did your concept of reality change? Like for example I became an atheist for a few months.

Kayley: I've become a lot more cynical I think. And a lot more sarcastic. I went through PTSD and panic attacks for a while because of my experiences from being restrained and drug reactions. So for a while I basically feared everybody.

Me: That's terrible.

Kayley: I felt like I had no future or no future worth anything.

Me: It's okay, I felt, still kinda feel the same way about the future.

Kayley: It's strange how some aspects of my PTSD remain, even though the clinical symptoms are gone. For instance, I'm paranoid about what drugs I'm getting. And I will never, ever take another dopamine antagonist. Period. End of story. Or a benzodiazepine. I had to be put under for the MRI I had before surgery and I must have asked the anesthesiologist several times over whether there were any benzos in the drugs. But it was all propofol so it was good.

Me: You certainly know your drugs.

Kayley: Ya I kinda had to. Once I figured out the doctors wouldn't do it for me. I eventually did a spreadsheet. Wrote down every drug I'd taken and the reaction if there was a bad one I googles to find out what kind of drug it was and within thirty minutes with the spreadsheet, drugs.com and Wikipedia I saw a pattern.

Me: Desperation calls for dedication.

Kayley: My brain doesn't like when its GABA is messed with or it's dopamine is blocked. And as long as I stay away from those medications I'll be okay. So no benzos and no antipsychotics. Or reglan. With my luck I'd get Tardive Dyskinesia (slow, repetitive movements) I was puking after taking Percocet in the hospital after surgery and I was like "Give me something but no dopaminergics, period. Since they use dopaminerigics for antiemetics also. Zofran, good stuff. Although that's a serotonergic, which I do okay with. I take Zoloft and melatonin.

Me: All these words I've never heard of, making me feel dumb (Laughs)

Kayley: (Laughs) No problem. So benzodiazepenes enhance the activity of this sort of inhibitory chemical in the brain called GABA or gamma butyric acid. And antipsychotics like Haldol or fluphenazine/pimozoide and their kin block dopamine in your brain. So they're called dopaminergics (dopamine+ergic meaning its acts on them) or dopamine blockers referring to how they block dopamine from your brain cells, or neuroleptics which is an old word neurologists seems to prefer to use it because it makes it sound a little nicer than saying they're putting somebody who's not psychotic on antipsychotics. Me: You certainly are a wealth of information.

Kayley: (Laughs) Ya most of it is from Google. Leave somebody alone with it and a terror and mistrust of their doctors and I'm what you get. I started googling everything after an ER doctor gave me the wrong drug.

Me: Holy shit that actually happened?

Kayley: They'd given me Ativan that made me go nuts, my brain doesn't like benzos/GABAergics which is what Ativan does. So they were like "we have to give her SOMETHING" and my mom tells them "She can't have fluphenazine". Doctor says "Oh this isn't fluphenazine, it's Prolixin" and gives it to me. Well after persuading them not to institutionalize me because I went nuts on Ativan and they wanted to keep me, and they did for thirty hours, although my parents were in the room the whole time because the hospital's psych ward was full and we were in this overflow room that had friggin rubber furniture, anyway we get home and I'm like "Did this really just happen?" and then my neck starts spasming to the side and my teeth start grinding because my jaw doing this weird side thing and it all really hurts. Hmmm ... not fluphenazine you say? Google and Drugs.com say different. Prolixin IS a trade name for fluphenazine.

Me: What a terrible doctor. Can't even check the medication.

Kaley: Yep so I had to go back to the ER, a different one of course, to get an IV because we ran out of benztropine at home.

Me: Jesus.

Kayley: At that point after two previous dystonic reactions we were keeping the antidote at home. Because, well, we seemed to need it an awful lot. Benadryl helps too although it was never enough alone to make my brain stop freaking out. I mean IV Benadryl might have worked but we don't have IVs at home. So after that I didn't really trust any drugs at all and got very sucked into researching it. This was three months into my exacerbation and I was fourteen and convulsing, hitting myself, swearing, and spitting. I was completely out of school because the principal was like "How is this going to work?" and my doctors were like "She can't go to school until we find something that helps." Spoiler alert: they wouldn't find anything that helps.

Me: See, early on my parents developed a mistrust of doctors and did a more "homeopathic" route. So I had a lot of creams, homemade concoctions, and bullshit herbal supplements.

Kayley: Oh we did that too. After Leckman, who's a researcher at Yale, recommend Chinese traditional medicine. Which didn't last long because the practitioner gave us this "tea" stuff but you had to boil these sticks and things and well I would have drunk it anyway but it was so awful I couldn't drink it. Then we tried acupuncture. I actually liked it. I hardly had any tics while the needles were in. Although overall it didn't help much but just that thirty minutes or so a week was awesome.

Me: I tried acupuncture once except I DID tic while the needles were in. Didn't end well.

Kayley: (Laughs) Oh I can't imagine so. Tics plus tons of needle? (Laughs) We also tried a myriad of supplements because one semi doctor thought it would do good things to the mitochondria in my brain or some shit. I was like on ten pills a day. Maybe more than that. And there was this really awful chalky creatine wafer stuff that was like impossible to swallow.

Me: I did this thing called a hyperbaric chamber. It was a six foot long, one foot wide tube that you had to lay in. Got very hot very fast. It was supposed to fill your body with oxygen. Not sure how that helps tics but whatever.

Kayley: Ya I haven't done that. Pretty much one of the only things I didn't try. There's something I wanted to bring up.

Me: Shoot.

Kayley: I saw in the *Cracke.com* article you had IVIG done?

Me: Ya the thing is for the first time it worked... for about two weeks.

Kayley: Wow must've been a good two weeks. We thought about PANDAS for awhile but after consulting my doctors and taking a few tests it didn't seem like that'd be it. I've also tried neuro feedback.

Me: Oh I did that too.

Kayley: I also tried hypnosis. Funny thing is after most of the medications failed the doctors at Yale were the ones to suggest the alternative medications because they didn't like the idea of DBS. He recommended electroshock therapy before DBS.

Me: Really? My doctors are the same way they wanted to try medication first. They thought DBS was too extreme. Which it is. It's brain surgery.

Kayley: Have you been on tetrabenazine/xenaxine? It's one of the last drugs they always want you to try before doing anything too "out there". It's a drug originally used for Huntington's Chorea, bad bad bad worse than parkinson's brain dying slowly type disease.

Me: No I haven't tried it. The pimozide worked for me surprisingly. Although it did cause severe depression for a few months.

Kayley: It has some promise for other movement disorders. It block dopamine indirectly. Personally I was never impressed with it. All it did was make me sleep all the time. I almost fell asleep in the pool at Tourette's camp if that says anything. And if I missed one dose it was tic city because I was in withdrawal.

Me: Tell me about Tourette's camp.

Kayley: Oh gosh it was awesome. Or at least was, until I tried to be a counselor in training. And then ... the whole .... "I have to be insanely careful because I will trigger huge attacks" thing kind of ruined everything. Like it's super noisy. If you've ever been around other people with Tourette's you know how that just triggers tics like crazy.

Me: Oh I can imagine.

Kayley: So I was having tons of attacks.

Me: Ya it's like a messed up chain reaction.

Kayley: And I didn't have my own wheelchair at the time so that sucked. Even with my service dog sometimes it was unbearable. I had to leave him in the cabin sometimes because it was so hot. This camp is in Georgia.

Me: Twist and Shout. If you know Brad Cohen. He's this teacher with Tourette's and he wrote a book *Front of the Class* and there's also a hallmark movie of the same name. Anyway he and other TS people in Atlanta started a camp. Brad's really cool although he's not at the camp anymore because he got promoted to principal. Although the actor who played him, Jimmy Wolk, still goes to the camp as a counselor.

Me: That's funny. I was going to name my book "Twist and Shout".

Kayley: Awesome (Laughs)

Me: My sister thinks I'm making fun of kids with Tourette's. How do you like it?

Kayley: "Twist" works for me, I tend to twist a lot.

Me: Just curious.

Kayley: Nah I like it. It's clever.

Me: Cool. Tell about your friends. Have they been a good support system for you?

Kayley: I don't have a lot in person friends. I am very active online though in the TS community Facebook page called Tic Talk. There's like two thousand people on there although most of them are parents and they tend to drive us with actual Tourette's kind of crazy.

Me: Huh. I've never heard of that.

Kayley: If you're not huge into Facebook it's hard to miss.

Me: I mean I have one but I never thought to reach out like you did. I think I was partly embarrassed. I didn't want to admit that I had Tourette's.

Kayley: I talk to several others with Tourette's including a couple of really good friends just about every day. Well "Talk" as in chat online. But you get the idea. Two of whom I finally got to meet with this spring when I went to New York for the first DBS appointment.

Me: Oh wow.

Kayley. It was so cool to finally meet them. Kind of weird too. When you only talk online you picture their voices in your head.

Me: And when you finally meet them it's so much different. But it's like I've known them my whole life.

Me: This may be a little hard to answer but how was your social life? Like how was all that high school bullshit but with a dash of Tourette's thrown in there?

Kayley: (Laughs) It sucked. I had like four friends in high school. Four. Part of that was because my entire first year of high school they wouldn't even let me go to school.

Me: Who wouldn't let you go to school?

Kayley: The administration, just like, barred me form class. They said with the swearing it was just too much.

Me: No shit?

Kayley: Yeah for real. I was so mad. And part of me was terrified of going to school afraid of how they'd react and stuff. The PTSD came into play again.

Me: That's amazing. It's not like you were purposely trying to upset anyone.

Kayley: These people telling you, you can't do something crucial to your future. My doctors were pushing for me to go back to school as well. Even Leckman said it's vital that I don't become a hermit and go out in front of people.

Me: When my tics were bad I never wanted to go out. Yet once I was actually out of the house and in a crowd I actually felt better.

Kayley: Well when we went to the local newspaper and had the TSA (Tourette's Syndrome Association) do an interview they suddenly turned their thinking around.

Kayley: My mom arranged for Susan Conners from the TSA to do a presentation on Tourette's Syndrome and tics at my school.

Me: How did that turn out?

Kayley: It went great. And the school gave out pamphlets to students. My ENTIRE school was educated about me. I don't think it could've worked out otherwise.

Me: Gee would've been nice if I had that happen. People probably wouldn't think I was just some weirdo.

Kayley: It was essential to me. I mean given all the racial slurs I used to yell and the fact that my school was a third minority. It... might not have gone very well ya know?

Me: Oh ya that couldn't have been good.

Kayley: My first year in school was my sophomore year since I was homebound all of freshman year. I had an attendant with me all the time. She pushed my wheelchair around after me if I was walking, although I think I ended up riding in the chair more than not because of the tics. And then there were my attacks. My attacks would last for hours sometimes. We ended up "borrowing" some gym mats from the cheer leaders and put them in one private are of the school we had found for me to retreat to. A closet office in the special ed room. I'd go there when I had an attack and just lie there convulsing until I passed out asleep, exhausted. My sophomore year I was either out convulsing on the mats or going home early more often than I was in class. It was brutal.

Me: What about your junior and senior year?

(Note: I am getting really tired of typing out "Kayley" over and over again so now I'm just going to type out "K" instead. Deal with it if you don't like it)

K: Now my junior year was a lot better. I had applied for a service dog and the organization told me they were ready to pair me with a dog. Mack. He was originally intended to do mobility stuff like pull my wheelchair, retrieve things, take things from me when I was about to hit or stab myself, and to lie on me during attacks to keep me from rolling into furniture and hurting myself. But it ended up when we lays on top of me the deep pressure does something good to my system. That and the whole puppy love thing. You know how getting absorbed into something helps tics? Well the first time he lay on top of me during an attack, we the call command across, and he like goes "across" me and lays down. The first attack lasted twenty minutes. The next attack lasted sixteen. And by the time training was over, which was two weeks long, the attacks, the movements, would stop almost instantly when he lay down on top of me. There's this principal in psychology called "operant conditioning" and basically I think my nervous system learned to chill out when the conditioned stimulus of him laying down on top of me is presented. It's the same sort of deal they try to teach you with relaxation.

Me: Makes sense.

K: I couldn't do deep breathing long enough because my tics were so horrific. I couldn't calm down enough during attacks to stop it. So Mack, pushes those buttons for me so to say. And the deep pressure helps my tics. He's like a giant teddy bear, he's a golden retriever so … you know how they are. Also interestingly, Leckman said that people who fall in love have their tics diminished significantly.

Me: Really? I've never heard of that before. I mean it kinda makes sense.

K: Everybody jokes that I'm in love with Mack. I mean he's my baby. Like having a kid. So I'm sure all the oxytocin, the feel good chemical in your brain, releases when you hug someone. That sort of warm and fuzzy feeling. Funny thing is he is so fuzzy there's fur everywhere now. For Christmas this year I got a Roomba.

Me: (Laughs) Well I'm glad that worked out for ya.

K: Thanks. Anyway back to my junior year. The hallways, being around all those people made me tic like crazy. I have sensory issues. Mack helped a lot during my attacks. It was probably my best year ever since my tics got bad.

Me: Well that's good to hear.

K: Back to my sensory issues. It's this rare condition called misophonia where certain sounds basically send you in this rage or fear state. And of me those noises were sniffing, throat clearing, coughing, snoring, etc. And they trigger my tics, make them really bad.

Me: Those were some of my early tics.

K: (Laughs) I know right? My dad's tics include throat clearing so that makes being around each other fun.

Me: Oh your dad has Tourette's too?

K: Well not diagnosed. But he had multiple motor tics as a kid. My brother has tics too although his are mild to moderate. His autism is a much bigger problem.

Me: I heard tics and autism sometimes go hand in hand, like OCD.

K: Yep, his autism is a much bigger deal than the tics though they are only mild to moderate at their worst. I was diagnosed with Asperger's actually. I had a lot of social anxiety when I was young. Which didn't exactly improve with the general mistrust of humanity and PTSD. And the whole "being the weird kid with Tourette's" sort of thing. The shrink I saw for a psych evaluation before the DBS debated me having Asperger's because the symptoms have improved. My main symptoms are social anxiety, awkwardness, I tend to monologue, and I get obsessed very easily. For example when I was going to get a new wheelchair, I researched endless hours online for over a year before finally settling on the right one.

Me: Could that just be OCD? Could you describe your obsessions to me?

K: (Laughs) They're kind of weird. My first ones were like scrupulosity. I was extremely religious as a child. Funny how that's changed now.

Me: Oh so was I.

K: Praying "wrong" was a trigger. So I had to do it over and over again until I got it just right. And in fourth grade we read this story about a mummy and I was terrified for a long time. I barely slept.

Me: It's ok when up until recently I checked my bed and closet for serial killers.

K: (Laughs) Same. Funny thing is I love horror now.

We talk about horror for some time. We talk about our favorite television shows and Kayley's venture into fan fiction. We got a little off topic (okay a lot off topic) so I asked her about her date with DBS.

Me: How are your tics after getting DBS?

K: I mean I still have attacks but they've been less frequent it seems and usually a bit shorter and more responsive to strategies.

Me: That's great to hear.

K: I'm not using the wheelchair anymore if that says anything.

Me: Yes that's saying a lot.

K: It's weird. I was obsessed with getting the perfect wheelchair, spent a year looking at different models, now I don't even need one. Well not perfect. The caster fork is bent thanks to one of my attacks.

Me: Wow I've broken cups before but I can't imagine breaking a whole wheelchair.

K: Yes my attacks unfortunately still happened while I was in the wheelchair. Driving it was a bitch. I'd crash into walls or even fall out of it sometimes. Like right now I'm only at two volts on my stimulators. And haven't had much programming yet. Only seven weeks out of surgery. Last Tuesday was the first day I could actually exercise.

Me: Tell me about DBS. Like how it works.

K: Annoying ass recovery period. And the whole thing sounds super friggin scary. But in my experience at least it was really not that bad. The whole time you're awake and they poke your brain with wires while your head is in a huge vice thing bolted in place and you have to tell them how you feel during it. But it actually went great. For me the most nerve wrecking part was waiting to see if they'd say they would approve me to have it or not. I only contacted them in like January. After I got kicked out of my anthropology class at college. Well not quite kicked out but they made me leave class and watch it via video feed. I did finish school, somehow, but it was tough.

Me: This is going to sound strange but how is it different for a girl with Tourette's? Like from the female perspective how does it differentiate?

K: Well there's the whole thing with your period. That sets me off pretty bad. And it's hard to apply makeup as well if you can imagine that disaster. But I think for a female there's a little more acceptance of tics. Like with males it's stigmatized, because the stereotype that males should just deal with it and "man up".

Me: Makes sense in a messed up way.

K: It's also funny when you go to Tourette's camp. There's like ten boys for every girl.

Me: Well ya it's more common in boys I believe anyway.

K: It is. But that didn't make camp dances any less awkward (Laughs).

Me: The big question is why does it affect boys more than girls?

K: Nobody knows. Something to do with sex linked chromosomal abnormalities probably. They're doing genetics research now. They've found, and I could be wrong about this, like two genes that are linked to Tourette's in like two families out of thousands they've tested. The whole thing is not a clinically homogenous entity. Meaning it's not one disorder with one cause but several forms of whatever the heck is causing it. And the fact that it doesn't respond to the same treatments for everybody and progresses different for everybody.

Me: You certainly know your stuff.

K: Too much time on my hands. Too much isolation. Too much Googling. That and I'm pretty obsessed with it. I love science. I love the idea of kicking Tourette's ass since it kicked mine so many times. I want to become a researcher and finally solve this problem that effects so many kids.

Me: Off topic a little, but do you ever smoke weed?

K: Nah, I wish man. The only drug that has ever really helped me was pure THC. What I took was actually legal in all fifty states. It's called dronabinol or marinol.

Me: Why did you stop taking it?

K: It seemed to stop working and just made me high. Like anxious high.

Me: Ah that'd do it.

K: One time I took like three pills at once and I had the worst trip ever (Laughs). I was so shaky and super anxious. And everything was going very slow yet really fast at the same time.

Me: I've been there. One time I ate an edible in the woods with my friends. We starred at a creek for an hour and then I vomited in my friend's car.

Me: What about alcohol? Worse or better?

K: I haven't tried it yet. I'm 19.

Me: Haven't snuck some around?

K: No! (Laughs) I can't imagine it making me feel good though.

Me: Well Kayley I just wanted to say thank your for talking to me today. I really learned a lot.

K: Don't mention it and thank you (Laughs). If you want there's a group on Facebook about DBS. It's run by the mom of a girl who had it done. It talks about what hospitals they went to, what part of the brain is being stimulated, etc. A lot of good information on that page, it's called "DBS for Tourette's" and it's really good to have this up there. Not many of us have had DBS and it's rare among the TS community.

Me: Thanks for sharing that Kayley. Good luck with your treatment.

Kayley sure did teach me a lot about my own disorder. Feeling betrayed by your own doctors can make a person very educated on their own.

There was something special about Kayley.

You have to respect someone whose been through so much and came out sane. I just wanted to point out though that just because so many things didn't work for Kayley doesn't mean that they work for you.

Tourette's is an odd thing. All I can recommend is that you find a trustworthy doctor and work with him/her to overcome your problem. This of course if you have Tourette's and are reading this. If you're one of those regular folks who are so privileged that they can control your movements then first of all: Fuck you.

Second: I'm sorry I didn't mean that. Thank you for reading this far.

Kayley's story is inspiring, and also makes me think about my own complaints.

I was sick.

But I was never THAT sick.

It brings me back to when I thought about ending my own life and how incredibly selfish that would have been and also would've made me look like a huge pussy.

Because compared to Kayley my journey was easy.

A walk in the park compared to what she went through.

So yes I feel guilty for having those thoughts.

And so should you.

There's a good chance that your life isn't exactly full of hardships compared to Kayley.

So whenever your self-esteem drops below zero, just be glad you don't need a brain surgery to stop hitting yourself.

THE TWITCHY PHILOSOPHER
OR:
HOW I STOPPED WORRYING
AND LEARNED TO LOVE LIFE

I've always been a little anxious of a person.

I've mentioned before how I started crying when I went through an existential crisis at age six.

One time I got drunk at a beach and jumped in the lake with my phone in my pocket.

I was upset for a week.

It was an easy fix.

Just get a new phone am I right?

But I couldn't let it go.

I couldn't get over it.

I couldn't get over the destruction of an inanimate object because it impeded my life slightly.

My life was different.

Change had occurred.

And I just couldn't handle it.

I didn't try to kill myself or anything over the phone.

But I did wear pajamas all day and sat in a slump for days watching television and not much else.

I get depressed quite easily.

And I'm positive there was a time you did to.

Or even currently are.

I don't care if you have Tourette's like me or your child does or what.

The world is kind of a shitty place sometimes.

But for large portion of it, it's not.

We just make it shitty for ourselves.

We put value in silly things and when things don't go our way we get upset.

Why should things go our way?

We are a group of individuals with no power.

We are members of a very young species.

We are not Gods.

We can't control every aspect of our fate.

Most of it ya, we do own.

You are in control for most of your life.

You get to decide what to do with your life.

You have so much choice and you don't even know it.

However sometimes shit just happens.

You lose your phone.

Your car gets stolen.

You wake up with Tourette's one day.

Someone you love dies.

You die.

Shitty things happen all the time.

The only thing you can do is adapt and roll with the changes.

I mean what's the alternative?

Kill yourself?

What does that really solve?

Let me tell you something personal.

(Like I haven't been doing that already)

I used to think about killing myself.

A lot.

Somedays it was the only thought that crossed my mind.

One day I sat on my bed and held a blade up to my own throat.

I wondered what it would be like to do it.

To just let it all go and give in.

I seriously thought about it.

But then I had an idea.

The idea was "What if this is it?"

As in, what if this is what my life would become.

No legacy.

Just dying on the floor.

To be forgotten eventually.

Pretty depressing thought, I know.

But that thought resonated with me.

And I put down the blade.

(It was a machete.)

(Why do I own a machete? When I turned 18 it was my first purchase as an adult. I remember going to Dick's Sporting Goods with my friends John and Omar and picking out my future zombie killing weapon. Side note: I was a stupid kid. Still kind of am. Anyway the cashier looks at my ID, looks at my stupid grinning face and says "It's your lucky day." So my first purchase as an eighteen year old wasn't cigarettes or porno like a normal eighteen year old. It was a deadly weapon. Cost me $20. Gives you a little more insight to who I am as a person.)

I put down the blade and thought about life for a while.

I thought about my life.

And how outrageous it was that I am here, as a person.

Think about life for a second.

How crazy is it that you are here, reading this book?

You were once a sperm.

I mean this in the most mature way possible just roll with it.

One sperm out of millions.

And then you were inside your mom.

And you beat millions of other of your little brothers and sisters to the egg.

And that egg got fertilized by you and there were no life ending complications from there until your birth.

Which also went on without a hitch.

You wouldn't be here reading if it didn't.

And it's not just you.

It's your parents births as well.

If your parents were different people then you wouldn't be here.

And your grandparents as well.

And your great grandparents.

And your great-great grandparents.

And you great-great-great grandparents.

Look I can fill like a thousand more pages of this because it would go on that long but I won't because that would be boring to read and I am not a crazy person.

You get the point, you're a smart cookie.

All of these people have such an unlikely chance of being born and yet they did.

Same goes for each of them growing up and not dying along the way and meeting that special someone and the exact moment they did and conceiving a child at the exact moment they did to carry one the genetic line.

It's pretty extravagant when you put it that way.

You really have a trillion in one chance of living at this point.

But it's not just that either.

It's all the things in history that lead up to this point as well.

Think about it: If World War II went differently your great grandparents may not have survived it and you wouldn't exist.

Or if your great-10x-grandmother was burned at the stake as a witch in medieval times you wouldn't exist.

Or if that meteor never wiped out the dinosaurs, you wouldn't exist.

So many things.

So many variables.

Really, you shouldn't exist.

But you do.

I've heard someone once say it's arrogant to think a loving God tailored you for a purpose.

I also heard the rebuttal, stating it's actually more arrogant to assume special little you came into existence out or pure chance.

I believe in a higher power, but I get it if you don't.

My point is: Don't kill yourself.

Ever.

If you do you slap your parents and your grandparents and your great grandparents right in the fucking face.

You tell them: "I realize that you all shouldn't exist and you all got together at the right time just to make me, but I'm not grateful with the gift of existing that you bestowed upon me. Fuck you."

That's the message you send when you kill yourself.

So please don't do it.

We live in a pretty wonderful universe to just go ahead and kill yourself.

You're wasting a precious gift.

And the outcome might be worse than your life is know.

(When I say "might be" I mean it will be. Much worse)

Let's say the classic version of God is real.

And so is heaven and hell.

Guess where you're going?

What makes you think you'll go to heaven for killing yourself?

According to the idea from Dante's Inferno, there are multiple layers of hell.

If you kill yourself, again according to the Bible, you get placed with all the murderers.

You really want to end up there?

That's basically prison.

You go to special eternity prison for killing yourself.

And it's like really hot there.

And I don't know what happens after you die.

I'm a twenty-something year old writer who once thought he was turning into a dinosaur when he was a little kid.

I have no real authority to tell you what's right and what's wrong.

But here's the thing.

Let's just say for the sake of the argument that the atheists are right.

And there is nothing after you die.

Is that really a better alternative to how you're living now?

Seriously?

Just emptiness.

Imagine how it was before you were born.

Ya, exactly.

That may seem peaceful to some people but I would rather live my life to the fullest and experience as much as possible before that happens.

You cut your life short and it's just nothing when it's over.

You miss out on so much.

You have no idea what the universe has in store for you down the road.

Anything can happen.

I do not have faith.

I am a very cynical person.

However even I sometimes have hope for the future.

Hope things will get better.

It's all I can do.

And for a while it's all I did.

All I could do was sit there and wait for things to get better.

And you know what?

Eventually things did get better.

After all you're reading a book that I wrote.

Clearly things work out for me in the end.

Or maybe they don't and you are literally the only person reading this.

Even if that is that case then I suppose I did something right.

Even if only one other person reads my stuff then that's a dream come true.

❦

That's all I really ever wanted to do.

To create stuff.

If there is a God then I get it.

The need to create.

The feeling of accomplishment you get when something you made gets recognized.

One time during my second year of college I took a creative writing class.

I'm sure I've mentioned this before.

But one day we had a contest.

Who can write the best story.

We were assigned partners and given a topic.

(The topic was racism)

We had to write a story that revolved around the topic and this was the one time we could write genre fiction.

Our teacher had a point.

If you couldn't write about the insanity of the real world, how do you expect to write about fantastic?

Anyway we my partner and I had some difficulty writing at first.

We couldn't agree on what to write about.

She, my partner, wanted to do something along the lines of genre fiction and I was already used to writing realistic fiction that I didn't want to switch over.

Eventually I gave in and we started brainstorming on science fiction and fantasy ideas.

We thought about our topic (racism, again) and thought about how can we make this elaborate and interesting.

We settled on robots.

Specifically about their struggle in a human dominated world.

So we shot ideas back and forth and started to piece together a story.

Do you want to read it?

You really don't have a choice cause I'm putting it in here anyway.

Well I suppose you still have the choice on reading it or not.

You could always skip over it.

But that would be a little unnecessary don't you think?

Anyway without further ado, here is my story.

Untitled.

UNDER THE RULING OF KAPERSKY VS. ISSACS, NO ARTIFICIAL PERSONS WILL BE ALLOWED BY LAW TO OWN OR OPERATE A MORTORIZED VEHICLE.
—New Constitution, Article 12, Section 7. 2045.

I have always been a worrier. Ever since my creation I have been chronically plagued by thoughts of death. People tell me that this is nonsense, they tell me I cannot die for I am not alive. But I still worry. And it is worry that brought the virus to my attention. A bug that was going around and causing malfunctions. I knew something was wrong when my right leg stopped working. The news said that motor errors were the first sign of the virus. My kind thinks before we act. We process data unlike your kind. But there was no process this time. Only action. I didn't want to die. I limped toward the nearest taxi and almost ripped the door off the hinges.

The driver wasn't pleased.

"You have five seconds to get out of my cab." He yelled.

I tell him: "Please sir, I require service. Please take me to the nearest mechanical station at 143rd and Antros Road."

"I don't serve your kind, get your metal ass out of the cab." The man raised a large pistol.

"Sir please I have no other options."

"I told you to get out, boy" The man motioned the gun toward me.

"Sir, if I don't receive treatment soon I will die anyway. The threat of violence does not scare me."

The man starred at me for a while. His eyes held a sort of hatred of me. Hatred that stemmed from confusion and fear.

The man spoke up again. "Look... the nearest station is still on the opposite side of town. I don't even think I have enough gas to get there."

"I will give you everything I have."

"I doubt your kind even has enough for one gallon of gas let alone a full tank."

"Sir, I do not wish to die."

"You don't have a soul. Man made you not God. You are not a real person. Why should I care> All your kind does is waste space and steal jobs from hard-working, God-fearing Americans."

"Sir ... I do not know if I have a soul. I do not know what a soul is. But I have memories. I remember coming into existence for the first time sixteen years, five months, three weeks, four days and twelve hours ago. I remember my first thought and my first action. The man who created me did it out of need for a son. Not for work. To fill an emptiness inside him. I have dreams, hopes, and desires. I love cooking for humans. I had dreamed of being a chef one day if I am ever allowed to be one. I have a right to live. You may not see it because I am different. But the right is there. You don't see that though. You see an abomination. Because I am different. Because I wasn't born like you were born. You have memories. You have dreams. You have hopes and desires. You have a right to live. We have more in common than we have in difference. You have a soul. And you say I do not. Tell me, why I shouldn't have the right to one?"

The man looked at me. His look of hate was replaced by one of sadness. He lowered his pistol and turned his head. "I lost someone once. The rescue bots said she couldn't be saved. That is was 'statistically impossible'. Your kind doesn't try. You just assume."

"We are not all alike. Please sir."

"Look ... I don't even know if we could make it. It's far away and we already wasted time."

"Can you at least try."

The man looked at the steering wheel. He took a deep breath and mumbled something under his breath. It sounded like a name. He shifted into gear and started to drive.

"Thank you" I said. I wanted him to know that. I wanted him to know I thought he wasn't like the others and that he deserved recognition. I wanted him to know that before I started to lose consciousness.

What did you think?

Did you like it?

I'm not sure why I'm asking, it's not like I'm going to get any feedback on this from you.

Personally, I hate the story.

I wrote it all by myself without any help from my partner.

True she may have come up with the ideas but in terms of physically writing down anything she did jack shit.

Turns out we ended up winning that contest.

We each won 25 extra credit points and $25 each.

I got paid for a story.

And it felt amazing.

It's what made me want to become a writer.

The feeling of creation.

I created a world separate of my own.

Does that sound over dramatic?

Yes.

But does it really?

I felt that writing was therapeutic in a way.

I could incorporate struggles I had in my own life into the story realm.

It felt good to write.

It felt like I was accomplishing something when all I was really doing was wasting my own time.

Why was I wasting my own time?

Because I wasn't going to actually finish this book.

Of course not.

It was something to do while I was bored of video games and nothing was on T.V.

I didn't have faith in myself to actually write a good story.

A big part of maturing is seeing your real life potential.

An immature person doesn't try to accomplish hard things.

A child doesn't try to climb the highest tree in the park. He goes for the smaller ones. He climbs the ones in his comfort zone.

Writing a novel wasn't in my comfort zone at nearly any point in my life.

But I did it.

How did I do it?

I didn't really intend to publish it.

No really, that was the secret.

I was confident if no one saw this, it would be forever in this perfect state.

Take that and apply it to people.

Let's say you had a person raised alone indoors, being taken care of by machines.

Would that child have any corruption?

Any problems?

I don't know, but I believe that child may be more at risk outside his quiet little room, although his potential it at zero.

If you don't take risks, you are safe.

If you are safe then you don't really grow.

Starting a business, talking to an attractive stranger, having a kid.

All super risky.

But why is that bad?

Risk is what life is about.

Risk is not just living, it's being alive.

I don't know why.

I may never know why.

I just know it is.

Maybe it's that little spark of creation put in us by something bigger.

Just a part of us.

I'm not sure if I agree that everyone should follow their dreams and passions.

If my dream is to explore a new galaxy by 2020, that's not going to happen.

Dreams may need to be tweaked a bit.

No one will ever go to another galaxy in 2020.

Maybe never.

But we can all explore one in the pages of a book we bought.

Or a book we write.

You need dreams.

You need reality.

Maybe those two things need you too.

CONGRATS, YOU FINISHED A BOOK!

Well here we are,

The end of the book.

Did you like it?

I hope you did, I spent a lot of time writing it when I could have been smoking weed and playing video games in my underwear.

Valuable time has been sacrificed to make this book.

What did we learn?

We learned that having Tourette's is something you shouldn't be dick about because it really fucking hurts and you look like an ignorant bitch when you mock someone for something they cannot help.

We learned that I am social outcast fuck-up.

But that I am also getting better!

We learned not to kill ourselves

(Seriously don't do it)

And we learned other people's perspectives and how they live their lives differently from your own.

We learned a lot of this literary journey.

I am glad you decided to take it with me.

I just hope you did indeed learn that stuff.

Life is beautiful.

And yes there are a lot of things that put us down.

Like disease and jerks and seeing loved ones suffer.

But there is always a silver lining to things.

Personally, having Tourette's changed who I was.

I still have a lot of changing to do, of course.

But I can say it made me a better person.

It made me more open to the world and I can see people and events and things through a different lens.

I look at life differently now.

I can see clearly now.

Everyone deserves respect.

Everybody.

Bullying each other is a pointless endeavor that leads to nowhere.

Whether you have Tourette's or any other disorder, are gay or straight, Atheist or Christian, black or white or any of the other races, religions, or sexual orientations out there.

You deserve respect.

Don't forget that.

Live your life the way you want to live it.

Treat others the way you want to be treated.

Wu-Tang Clan ain't nothing to fuck with.

Goodnight. Go read another book now.

FINAL WORDS

In case you were curious about my 26 year old thoughts while reading my 20 year old thoughts, to say I was finally blessed with maturity is to say the very least. Various factors have contributed to this:

- In 2015, shortly after this book was published, I had dropped out of university and checked myself into a psychiatric ward. I believed I spent 4 days there, however I was told it was 2 weeks. That is something I will never fully comprehend, nor do I want to.
- In early 2016, I fixed my connection with God and it has made my life several magnitudes better. I do not believe I am being rewarded so to say, I believe I now can see the reward was with me all along.
- In the summer of 2017, I tried an herbal supplement that made me several times worse for a week, and then zero tics for 2 months. I only stopped taking them in the fall of 2017.
- September 2017 I underwent Deep Brain Stimulation. It has altered my psyche to the point where I can go to work without hiding in the bathroom, I can approach people in public and talk elegantly and with confidence, and I can finally enjoy sitting still in complete silence.

The procedure was so far the most important event in my life. I could think coherent thoughts without second guessing or regretting everything I said and did.

There are many things that I did not include for personal reasons, however they had a clear presence in creating the mindset of the man you just read about. For one, after my tics manifested in something far more noticeable than clearing my throat, my mother wanted to kick me out of the house. It was only for the intervention of my father that I'm not living in a homeless shelter. He has been the one who researched everything. Some things didn't work, that doesn't mean he doesn't deserve credit. Frankly, despite being there for me for everything, while I was writing this book, I could not stand him. Everything he did annoyed me. I sincerely believe that all of the negative things in my life caused me to have a mental shattering of my reality. Losing time, having disturbing thoughts and dreams, overall irrationality. All things that have happened. It was only a few years ago that I realize the gift of having a father like him, I can only hope I am a fraction as good to my own kids.

Thanks Old Man.